THROUGH HIM, WITH HIM, IN HIM

Through Him, With Him, In Him

Meditations on the Liturgical Seasons

Ruth Burrows

EDITED, WITH FOREWORD AND LINE ILLUSTRATIONS, BY ELIZABETH RUTH OBBARD, ODC

Sheed & Ward

London

ISBN 0–7220–9080–3

Published in Great Britain in 1987 by
Sheed & Ward Limited
2 Creechurch Lane,
London EC3A 5AQ

Book production by Bill Ireson

Filmset by Fakenham Photosetting Ltd, Fakenham, Norfolk
Printed in Great Britain by A. Wheaton & Co. Ltd, Exeter

Contents

CONFERENCES FOR ADVENT AND CHRISTMASTIDE

CONTENTS

CONTENTS

List of Illustration Plates

(The line illustrations which appear throughout the book are by Elizabeth Ruth Obbard, ODC.)

Foreword

The Christian life revolves around the liturgy, and perhaps this is even more intensified in Carmel, where the seasons of Advent and Lent are completely integrated into a lifestyle in which the rhythm of fast and feast is interwoven with the cycle of the Church's year.

During Advent a hush of expectancy seems to fall upon the whole monastery, and the heart thrills as the first of the Advent antiphons is intoned in the Choir. This is a Marian season *par excellence*, culminating in the Midnight Mass of Christmas, prolonged by joyful singing, community companionship, log fires and festive cakes; all of which combine to make this a feast of homely light and warmth in the dark of winter.

Lent on the other hand opens with a fast day. The Gospels and the Offices of the season stress the call to repentance and renewal. But the soul is spring-cleaned and rinsed in the clear air rather than in dark gloom. Burgeoning new life pushes through the hard earth of the enclosure garden until it seems that the whole of nature is glorious in gold and green to greet the great feast of the Resurrection. During the Easter Vigil Baptismal promises and religious vows are renewed, and each one emerges from Mass in her white mantle, symbolic of the Baptismal robe, ready to mingle with her companions after the solemnity of the Sacred Triduum when liturgically each has died with Christ to rise to new life in Him.

In such a setting, conferences naturally follow closely the main themes of the liturgy; and here I have chosen a selection of Meditations and talks given by Ruth Burrows to her Carmelite community. Although they were delivered primarily with her sisters in mind, they are equally valid for all who try to live a full Christian life in tune with the Church's seasons of grace.

Lastly, I have included an article suitable for the feast of St Teresa on 15 October. As 'Mother of Carmel' she remains always an inspiration and guide to all who seek to follow in the ways of prayer, whether it be in an enclosure or in the midst of secular life.

Elizabeth Ruth Obbard, ODC

Acknowledgements

The scriptural quotations are taken from liturgical texts and the Divine Office translated jointly by R.B. and W.M.B. Several ideas expressed in this book are also due to W.M.B. whose deep spiritual insight has been a source of continual inspiration. The concluding chapter, Sustained Passion, was first published in *Mount Carmel* in 1982.

The illustration plates are reproduced by kind permission of the following:

Archivi Alinari (Galleria Palatina), Florence: *Granduca Madonna* (Raphael);
The Frick Collection, New York: *Polish Rider* (Rembrandt);
Kunsthistorisches Museum, Vienna, *The Way of the Cross* (Brueghel);
Museo Civico di Padova: *Nativity* (Giotto);
Museo dell'Opera del Duomo, Florence: *Florentine Pietà with Nicodemus* (Michelangelo);

Museo di San Marco, Florence: *Dominic at the foot of the Cross* (Fra Angelico);

Museo Nazionale del Bargello, Florence: *Pitti Madonna* (Michelangelo);

The National Gallery, London: *St Catherine of Alexandria* (Raphael);

The National Gallery of Art, Washington, D.C.: *Christ by the Sea of Galilee with Peter and the Apostles* (Tintoretto);

The National Gallery of Scotland, Edinburgh: *Christ in the house of Martha and Mary* (Vermeer);

Rijksmuseum, Amsterdam: *The Milkmaid* (Vermeer).

Conferences for
Advent
and
Christmastide

Come Lord Jesus

In accordance with our nature, nations and families have their times and seasons for days of special celebration. This specialness is sacramentalised in the Church's year. She too has red-letter days, seasons marked out in a special way to commemorate God's saving, life-giving love.

Are we right in claiming that God offers Himself more fully at these times? That the living water of grace is flowing even more abundantly? The wise answer is, I think, that as human beings we need to think so, and therefore it *is* so. The Church, in this manner, educates us in a more concentrated way, provides a more intense stimulation to faith so that, if we respond, we are better prepared for the Lord to give Himself more fully to us.

Advent is one of those special times as a season of preparation for the Feast of Christmas.

Our whole life is an advent, a time in which the Lord is coming. Although He has already come to each one of us, He has not fully come. A period of the Church's year is therefore set apart to, as it were, dramatise this situation.

We are to be as though He had not come. We identify with the waiting ages for whom He had not come. By entering into their condition, making our own their aspirations, their hopes, we are moved to desire His coming more and more; we purify and prepare our hearts. This dramatisation is sacramental – full of content – 'The Lord is coming,' the Church announces, 'Prepare your hearts to receive Him.'

First and foremost we must affirm our faith in the efficacy of the liturgy. This is no empty play-acting. God is here at work. He *is* coming as He has never come before. This is a wholly *new* Advent for us.

Let the piercing cry of the trumpet resound within our hearts:

> See, we have a God; see we have a Saviour!
> Oh see, our God is coming, coming in all His strength.
> He will be king, His throne will be compassion.
> I will pledge myself to you forever, my deep love for David will stand eternally sure. See, I am giving you all the earth to show them who I am; you will teach them and bring them to Me.
> Look, from afar the Lord is coming, and earth is shining with His light.
> Your heart should break for joy, daughter of Sion. See, your king comes. Can you be afraid any more? With eager love your Saviour comes.

On and on they go, the beautiful words assuring us of God's closeness, His desire to be our Emmanuel, our Saviour, our Love.

But faith in His coming does not grow of itself. We have to nourish our faith, exercise it. We don't sit idly at home waiting for His arrival – we must run out to make Him welcome. We must question Him: 'Are you He?' We must ponder the sacred texts, try to discover their meaning, receive their message.

There has to be effort in our daily living. We must climb the mountain heights where the God of Jacob makes His home, for we want Him to teach us how to love Him; we want to follow where He leads.

We must move into the shadowy mists of detachment. Far on the horizon see, God appears, and 'His coming spreads a mist over all the earth'. We should want this silencing, shadowing mist, that cuts us off from unnecessary things – things that are not Him for us. We cannot truly see them until He comes, so it is better to live in the mist – detachment, silence of desire – accepting the mystery. We must shroud our souls in Advent mist.

It may be, and in my experience often happens, that instead of the inner silence we so desire, our emotions are upset and our thoughts tend to run off. We can feel very discouraged about this lack of inner peace, but there is no need to be. This is merely temptation, the cross. In no way do these feelings come between God and us provided we quietly resist, and bear with ourselves sweetly and patiently. It may be, in fact, a far deeper Advent in that we realise our immense *need* of a Saviour – and what a blessing that is!

> I have thrust you into the furnace of your poverty out of love. Only so can you receive me, only so can I give you myself.
> You can only share my glory when you know it is not your own.
> For a moment, for a little while, I have had to withold myself from you; but never has my heart felt anything but compassion.

So let us enter into the mystery of Advent with profound

faith and eager desire, believing that God is offering Himself in fulness as never before. It is a special moment in our lives.

He will come. He has pledged His solemn word. Be watching constantly, for when He does come He comes with impatient love. You must wait a little yet, but only for a little, and then He will be here as He has promised.

Martha and Mary

Martha and Mary are the same woman. Martha is our natural, egotistic self. Mary what we are to become, what we are potentially; Martha is the centre of the picture, thrusting herself forward so that even our Lord is pushed a little to one side. She demands to be noticed, she matters so much to herself.

That is what we are all like until we allow Jesus to transform us. We really do see ourselves as the centre of the world, and everything else is viewed from this angle. It is our nature to be like that.

But as Christians we have deliberately set ourselves against this egotism. We want to put God in the centre where He truly belongs. Mary is the image of what we are to be. Mary is oblivious of herself, she is absorbed in Jesus. For her, He is the important one. In the picture she seems the insignificant one, yet in His eyes she is the treasure. He points her out as such.

We have to keep telling ourselves when our Martha rises

up indignantly to demand attention, to demand her rights: 'I am not important – You are important my Lord and Love. Take me from myself, give me to Thee.'

This attitude is carried deep into our prayer life itself, our direct relationship to Him. There too I learn that He is the important one. All my desire must be to enthrone Him in my heart, to hear His word, to do it. I do not demand to be consoled, to feel satisfied, to have a blissful time. Nor do I pray and work as if it were for me to transform myself, for me to be God. I have to recognise that I have nothing whatever to give Him but my trust and self-surrender – this is the food He delights in.

CHRIST IN THE HOUSE OF MARTHA AND MARY *Vermeer*

Our Healing Sun

No one can give herself to the liturgy of Advent without being made aware that a sense of sinfulness is being forced upon us:

> Deliver us from our sinfulness; break the chains that bind us captive: bring us out of darkness into light. Come, come!

This urgent cry is for what? To set us free. Free from what? Sin. No exceptions are allowed. The whole people is sinful, and each individual calls out for his own personal deliverance and for that of the whole human race.

But there is nothing depressing in this cry for deliverance and the deep consciousness of sin which prompts it, together with the conviction that we are quite powerless to deliver ourselves. 'For what man can pay his own ransom . . .?'

The cry the liturgy puts on our lips is a cry not of despair but of absolute hope – the certain hope that God will come and save us. He is by nature a coming God, always in movement towards His sinful creation, running to it with outstretched arms to enfold, to wipe away all tears, banish fear and haunting guilt, affording us utmost security in His forgiving love.

Some may feel that I speak too often of sin, rub it in too much. Others point out that what we need is encouragement, we are too aware already of our own miseries. But are we? Often what we are meaning and what we are confusing with an awareness of *sin* is self-disgust, self-disillusionment, which nearly every human being suffers from.

We have an image in our mind's eye of what we are like, or would want to be like, or think we are really meant to be like, and we fall short of it. We 'lose face' in our own eyes, and perhaps in the eyes of others. This makes us miserable and discouraged; and therefore we say we are in need of encouragement – not of having our deficiencies rubbed in more and more.

But this has nothing in common with what the liturgical texts are talking about and trying to induce in us. *Accepted* humbly, recognised for what it is – wounded self-love – our self-disgust can become a stepping stone to true sorrow for sin.

What we bewail is largely our human poverty, and this our Lord has no intention of taking away. This is what *we* would like to have removed from us. We are often far more concerned with this than with sin, and while we are occupied with it, battling against it, wringing our hands over it, we cannot be shown where real sin lies.

An awareness of our *real* sinfulness is part of holiness. You simply cannot have holiness without it, for it is the inevitable effect of God's closeness; and this is why true sorrow for sin is never morbid, depressed. It carries with it the certainty of forgiveness.

The liturgy assures us that the Lord comes precisely to heal our blindness. To a great extent, perhaps wholly, we choose how much we see. We cannot receive God unless we are prepared to see ourselves, our lives, our past and present as they are. Half-consciously we know this revelation would be terrible, so we make a choice not to see, or not to see too much.

Come and enlighten us, Sun of holiness. Show us our sloth, our pride, our shirking of the demands of life, our evasions. Reveal to us our sinfulness in the light of your mercy, and then we shall be healed and know perfect joy.

Our Lady's Advent

Our Lady is so close to God, yet she stands before us in all her glory to show what marvels God will accomplish in us, what heights, what nearness to Himself, if we but give ourselves to Him as she did, and allow Him to work in us.

She is God's most perfect design, the most perfect image of Christ Jesus. She submitted herself without reserve to God's action, carried out with unswerving fidelity all those things He had prepared beforehand for her life, whether little or great.

From moment to moment Mary looked for God's guidance and followed one step at a time. She embraced with all her heart whatever He willed or permitted. Her life was a continual 'fiat' to His operations. She sought only to please Him, to be docile in His hands, whether what He asked was painful or sweet. In fact all *was* sweet because it was Love's will.

Mary passed from one duty to another – from prayer to work, from work to repose, with the same tranquillity and singleness of purpose; ever hand in hand with the Beloved, her eyes upon Him. She accepted all with the same simple, unquestioning love. She did not ask to understand, to see the pattern of her life, to know what torments were in store. That was God's affair, not hers.

Every Christian life must be a contemplative life over-flowing in loving sacrifice. A Christian knows, loves and serves. Let us learn from Our Lady how to co-operate with the divine action. Let us learn to recognise it always and everywhere in hidden ways – its majesty obscured by lowli-ness, humiliation, suffering. Let us discern it too in the condition of our bodies: in weariness, aches and pains, as well as in a feeling of well-being. God's action is always there. He is always carrying out His purpose of deifying us.

We must have unshakeable faith in Divine Providence directing our lives. In the measure in which we surrender to God, in like measure does His loving providence surround us. We must have an ardent faith in His constant care, never ceasing to trust in His love.

> Fear not for I have redeemed you;
> I have called you by name, you are mine.
> When you pass through the waters I will be with you;
> and through the rivers, they shall not overwhelm
> you.
>
> ISAIAH 43: 1, 2

What greater joy can there be, what greater glory than that we should seek to glorify our Creator by being what He wants us to be? Each has her own special path to the goal. Only by being true to our own unique calling can we glorify the Lord.

God is in the simple, the routine, the uneventful, the drab things of life. It is there that we encounter Him and can, if we will, embrace Him as did Mary, for He is Emmanuel – God with us. Our task is to be with Him – always.

Room for God

In the weeks of Advent the Church is employing all her artistry, all her richest symbolism, to stimulate us towards understanding what God is offering. Every tiny particle of Scripture the Church chooses carries its own message. If we use these riches we long for the gift of God; we long to see Jesus.

But this stimulation of desire is only a means and not an end. We can throb with joyful expectancy; we can experience rapture as Christmas approaches, yet it may have no spiritual significance.

It is not enough for Jesus to come. We must be empty to receive him.

With sorrow Scripture points out that there was no room at the Inn. He had to turn aside and go elsewhere. His own received him not.

No awareness of wanting can assure us of real desire. Real desire is only shown by being changed.

Unless the graces of Advent and Christmas change us,

lead us to rid ourselves of self, then Jesus' coming is of no avail.

The condition for His reception is room. There must be room in our inn, and the rival that fills up space is no other than ourselves.

All that matters is to make space for God by embracing His will.

Where personal desires and self-will least abound there dwells the Lord most fully.

Eager Longing

We must awaken in our hearts an eager longing for all God wants to give. We have image after image in Scripture of His abundance. He contains all that our poor, sinful, blind, weak, grieving being needs. He is all – our shelter, our healing, our food, our delight.

We have received the first-fruits of the Spirit but not the harvest. Areas in us are untouched by Jesus . . . where His kingdom has not come in us. The Church wants us to stand conscious of our unredeemed state. In each of us are areas of dark confusion and chaos. Let us understand this and know that it is the weakness of our sight that hides it from us. We do not see what God is asking of us because we are too feeble and ungenerous to respond.

We must pray this Advent as we have never prayed before for perfect conversion, which will lead to redemption. Hold out to Him our chaos. Ask Him to transform us at whatever cost. Ask for the sight which sees Him when He comes, and for the strength to respond to His demands to move into fuller life. We are part of a violent, dark, chaotic world. In the measure that His peaceful kingdom comes within us, the darkness and chaos of the world diminishes.

All who call themselves Christian have an intellectual knowledge that Jesus has already come. Reciting the Creed sincerely we say, '. . . and in Jesus Christ, His only Son, our Lord; conceived by the Holy Spirit, born of the Virgin Mary, suffered under Pontius Pilate, was crucified, dead and buried. On the third day He rose again . . .' With all Christians we partake of the great sacrament of salvation.

But what of our own *personal* faith-knowledge that He has come?

> 'Happy the eyes that see what you see
> the ears that hear what you hear.'

But do we *really* see? Do we *really* hear? Or does our knowledge remain more or less intellectual?

Is the Mass, the great sacrament of salvation, of union with Jesus, the true centre of our lives? Do we really live it? Throughout our day are we intent only on being one with Jesus in doing the Father's will, being surrendered to Him? Or are we as often as not concerned with ourselves, our will, our desires, our status? We can soon know – if we want to be honest with ourselves.

It doesn't matter how great may be our intellectual or emotional appreciation of the Mass if our lives are not a continual Mass.

> My meat is to do the will of Him who sent me.
> I seek not my own glory
> I am about my Father's business.

How true is this of us? Yet this is what redemption means

. . . to be set free from self in order to be free for God. All the grace is there, for us to use or not. The sacrament of Reconciliation is ours, whereby we can expose ourselves to the profound action of God which alone can attack the deep, secret roots of sin. God is at work continually in us, delivering us from selfishness through the difficulties of each day . . . within, without. Do we miss these opportunities?

Everything about us should be revealing our faith that Jesus has come – is coming – affecting our inmost thoughts, our attitudes, our words, our actions. But, by and large, faith is weak. We live by what we perceive, what we feel, our subjective experience. We take *this* as reality.

But faith contacts the real world – what *is*. Faith never opts out of the world of service for it sees its deepest meaning. It sees that all has changed fundamentally and it lives by that knowledge.

Our Lady lived so. She lived from this certainty. The two feasts representing the beginning of her existence, and its end understood as fulfilment – Immaculate Conception and Assumption – show us Mary as the one fully saved, the one who opened herself to God's redeeming grace. A whole world of increasing holiness lay between her Immaculate Conception and her Assumption, yet at each stage all that there was of her was open to the Father, saying 'Yes' to His salvation in Jesus, no matter what the darkness and pain.

God's eager longing is to give us His perfect kingdom which is Himself. The Advent season is a time for a tremendous revival of hope.

Do I really believe He will give me, even me, absolutely everything? Blest are you if you believe, for most certainly everything the Lord has promised will come true.

Each One a Priest

This is Mary the priest. Even her garments are priestly. With utmost gravity and resolution, her whole being responding to her vocation, she offers her new-born Child to His Father. It was for this she bore Him; she knows it, He knows it and they look into one another's eyes with perfect understanding. They are one in dedication, trust and sacrifice. She reaches out to Him in His littleness and helplessness, swaddled as He is in the bonds of love.

Each of us is priest. Each of us has the responsibility and privilege of Mary to offer Jesus to His Father. This means, in practice, offering myself. I offer Jesus by offering myself in union with Him, my own substance hour by hour, drop by drop to become His substance. This is the Mass. This is why I exist.

Giotto gives a picture of how I must live, fully aware of the responsibility that rests upon me and acquitting myself of it with unremitting seriousness.

How lonely the Mary of this picture! No one can help

NATIVITY *Giotto*

her, not even holy Joseph. The task is hers and hers alone. No one can live my life for me; no one can relieve me of one atom of responsibility for the way I live my life, for what I make of my life.

We can learn something from Joseph too. He knows he can't help Mary directly. He knows an awful mystery is taking place between Mary and God. He doesn't attempt to intrude, doesn't fuss around trying to be important in that mystery. Rather, he sits quietly by, available if needed. But we know that his silent, loving, reverent presence is, in fact, supporting Mary. This is how we must be before the mystery of God surrounding another.

The Music of Birth

What if we had not been given the Infancy Gospels of Luke and Matthew? What if we had met our Lord only as a splendid adult? Revelation would not have been complete. True, we would have known that once He was a child, but the fact that in no way was our attention drawn to it would lead us to assume that it was not important:

As it is, God has taken care that our attention *is* drawn to it in a big way. Herein – in the fact of His human birth, infancy and childhood; in the fact that He had a human mother who looked after Him in a human way; that He was a member of a basic family unit – is a special revelation of who and what God is.

'The God who made light shine out of darkness has shone in our hearts.' He gives us a knowledge of Himself, a shining knowledge of Himself, in the face of this little child – in the picture of this little child in His mother's arms.

This revelation calls for our deepest meditation, and no other season of the year holds so many helps for our reflection. It is a season rich in poetic imagery and appeals to the tenderest human experiences and emotions.

Easter is pure light; white light beyond our ability to see. The Resurrection is something we cannot imagine, cannot write hymns about, cannot paint. It is supernatural, belonging to the dimension of light inaccessible. Christmas is that pure light broken up into a thousand rays, and we are meant to hold up this prism, turning it this way and that, so that we come to a knowledge of the pure light that is Easter.

Easter can mean nothing to us unless we have first lived with its reflected light in the mysteries of our Lord's earthly life.

What a multitude of pictures about the Babe and His mother! What a wide range of art, what a multitude of songs! There are poems, ballads, carols – encompassing what is little more than a mere lullaby that any mother might sing to her baby, to highest theology. One look at the Child and away one soars:

> Hail the heaven-born Prince of Peace, Hail the Son of Righteousness
> God from God, Light from Light, Begotten not created . . .

There are tender, meditative lyrics often sung from the point of view of His mother, pondering in her heart, anticipating the passion. Others express sheer jubilation, or are contemplative in nature.

> All the world's delight in swathing bands is bound.
> *O Patris caritas – O nati lenitas* . . .

Hardly any meaning; just a fragrance of the Love expressed in this mystery and the soul is carried away.

It is the same with painting. Some great pictures of the

Mother and Child are little more than a pure and beautiful mother cradling her baby. Others are almost cold in their austerity and detachment from the human scene. In early mediaeval times Mary is often shown lying on a couch gazing ahead, while her Infant is behind her, laid on an altar. We need this vast range – each, even the most superficial, is telling us something about God.

In the mystery of Christmas and in all that Christian love has built around it, we have a facet of God that is absolutely indispensable to a true knowledge of Him.

'Holy, holy, holy . . . I am a man of unclean lips and dwell among a people of unclean lips . . . No one can ever see God and live . . . Depart from me for I am a sinful man O Lord.' This profound sense of God as the utterly Holy and transcendent One can never be lost. But an awesome sense of deity is not the only revelation of the One True God. He is Love, offering intimacy. So we can sing Him lullabies.

The Great 'O' Antiphons

(Sung at Mass and Vespers on the days preceding Christmas.)

17 December
O WISDOM, O holy Word of God, the whole created universe lies throbbing in your strong and gentle hand. Come show us how to live.

18 December
O SACRED LORD of ancient Israel, who showed yourself to Moses in the burning bush, who gave him the holy law on Sinai mountain. Come stretch out your mighty arm to set us free.

19 December
O FLOWER OF JESSE'S STEM every eye is held by you, every prince of foreign power bows down in silent worship to your beauty. Come, let nothing keep you from our rescue.

20 December

O KEY OF DAVID, O royal power of Israel, controlling at
your will the gates of heaven. Come, break down the prison
walls of death, and lead your captive nation into freedom.

21 December

O SUN AT MORNING, O brightness of the everlasting light.
Come with all your holy sunlight where we lie in darkness
and in death.

22 December

O KING OF ALL NATIONS, the only joy of every human heart,
O Keystone of the mighty arch of man. Come and save the
creature you fashioned from the dust.

23 December

O EMMANUEL, God who lives with us to rule and guide, the
nations of the earth cry out with longing. Come and set us
free, our Saviour God.

You Are My Father

'And suddenly there was with the angel a multitude of the heavenly hosts praising God and saying, "Glory to God in the highest, and on earth peace to men who are God's friends."'

A rainbow of light and jubilant song spans our earth, and there are tidings of great, immense, immeasurable joy. Not vague rumours from an unreliable source, but a word, a covenant; tidings from God Himself swearing by His own being, His own fidelity – swearing eternal, everlasting friendship to all people.

And what is the immediate cause of this heaven-rending rapture; where the focus of this overwhelming joy? In a small, insignificant corner of the vast universe a little child has emerged from the womb and now lies helpless in a manger. What is the significance of this particular child? Moment by moment, through countless ages, babies are born, but the heavens are not rent and vocal in acclaim.

'He shall say to me, "You are my Father,"' (Responsorial

26

psalm, Christmas Midnight Mass.) The whole significance lies here. At last, at long last, God has His heart's desire; God is able to be what He is – Father. At last He can express His inmost nature: self-expending, self-donating love.

Hitherto the ocean of love has been pent up, held back by the resistance of hearts unable or unwilling to receive its flood. Here at last is a human heart that can and will receive it, whose whole existence is for that, to be a receptacle for the self-communicating love of God. But in receiving Love in its fulness the human heart will break; and through its rending will become, as the rock of old, a fountain of living waters for us all – living waters which are the outpourings of divine love.

This is God's glory, glory in the highest – that He should communicate Himself fully to the lowest; that each of us should receive to our full capacity the love He longs to bestow. It is possible now because of this little Child.

'He shall say to me, "You are my Father."' The entire mortal life of Jesus can be expressed as learning to say with ever fuller truth 'You are my Father.' Saying it not merely with His lips, not merely with the movements of His heart, but in His daily living, in His whole life. Jesus in Himself, in His very being *is* that cry, 'You are my Father!' That is why He is Son. That is what it means to be Son.

From the moment of His birth it begins: 'Glory to God in the highest' – because a tiny child is wailing in a manger, wailing as all infants do, 'with no language but a cry.' Yet even this unreflective cry coming from the newborn Babe is an affirmation of God's Fatherhood.

The helplessness, the dependency, the need, the pain this Child's cry embodies, symbolises in fact our basic condition, and is ultimately a cry to the Source of our being, our Origin, our Sustainer, our Rock, our only Fulfilment. In this holy Child the cry is already the inarticulate crying of the Spirit knowing the deepest nature, the deepest need of man, and crying with infallible assurance in its answer.

As the Child comes into reflective consciousness, as He grows physically, emotionally and intellectually, His sonship becomes a consuming reality, the passion of His life. 'You are my Father' is the unremitting, impassioned cry of His heart. This is expressed in unswerving practical devotion, summed up as fulfilling His Father's will. He received the Father's immense, self-sacrificing love into His human heart until it crushed Him.

You Are My Son

'You are My Son' . . . Jesus can only say with His life 'You are my Father,' because the Father has already called Him 'my beloved Son.' Jesus lives to the full the sonship already given Him.

'Glory to God in the highest and peace to men.' Here is perfect fulfilment because God is our Friend, our Father. He bestows sonship on us, begets us in Jesus. Do we live out the sonship thus bestowed? The tidings of immense joy are for you, for me, for each one without exception – for *all* people. Each of us may say 'You are my Father'. If we would be truly human, if we would give glory to God, our lives *must* say it.

It is easy to make general statements. Our living of sonship, our affirmation of God's fatherhood is a moment by moment business. Fatherhood means nothing unless it is exercised at every moment of our lives, and we must recognise it and respond. We need enlightened eyes of the heart to pierce the disguises, to say 'Yes, You are my Father' in the *now*. There is only one point, so to speak, where God is for us, and that is the *now*.

How readily we would escape from the *now* – into what we think should be, to what may be, to what has been, to what is coming. How much energy and attention we waste worrying over the past, being anxious and doubtful and full of fear for the future. 'I can't go on like this'; 'I can't cope with this day after day'; 'If I surrender to God there is no knowing what will be asked', etc. etc. All that is unreal. God isn't in it.

He is with me *now*; quietly, unobtrusively asking me to receive Him, to recognise Him. *Now* in this one little circumscribed moment I can say 'Yes, Father.' Such a poor little 'yes'; no grandiose certainties that I will never do this again, never commit that fault again – no dreads and despairs that I cannot be faithful. Only a little 'Yes' *now*. And the 'Yes' may be no more than, 'I want to say "Yes", even though at this moment I feel I can't say it fully.' But that *is* 'Yes'! That is to live in my poverty relying only on Him to see me through, to enable me to say 'Yes' – to do what *I* can't – be faithful unto death.

Oh, how simple it is, that poor little 'Yes' in the *now*; not in the future, not even an hour ahead, but *now* – and yet it is all that is required for God to give Himself entirely. This is to live sonship, total dependency, our whole life affirming 'You are my Father.'

I cannot think of anything more important for us than to work at establishing the conviction that God is Father. If only so much of the time and energy we expend on ourselves, our moods, our imaginary world were devoted to a constant alertness to the glorious transforming truth 'You are my Father' and its reply 'You are *my son*.'

Giving is Receiving

Mary is a most beautiful woman, but her beauty is not adventitious. It flows, not merely from beauty of line, the perfection of moulding and colour, but from her radiant spirit, the spirit of a perfect woman, one who has said a full-hearted 'Fiat' to what being a woman means. All love, strength, gentleness, tranquillity, vibrant with compassion, the Virgin Mother holds her Child – but holds Him for others.

There is no background to this picture; no thing and no one is there but the Mother and the Child. And yet we become aware that there is another present, off the picture. Mother and Child are looking, not at one another but at me, with a sad, serious, loving gaze.

The Child is not clinging to His Mother; He seems to be saying: 'She is all I want her to be; she has received all I want to give and I can love her to my heart's content. But you won't let me love you. I want to love you into becoming like her.' Mary herself, having entered so deeply into His heart, looks out at me with calm and holy wisdom. She can teach me all I need to know.

My sorrow should not be that *I* can't get close to God. The thing that matters is that God can't come close to me, can't have what He wants from me, and because I resist Him I keep Him from others. We never have God for ourselves alone. We must not be over-absorbed in our relation to Him, but, like Mary, be always offering Him for and to others.

GRANDUCA MADONNA   *Raphael*

Born of Mary

Let us turn our gaze upon the Babe, not as our little brother, but as one who shows us what the Father, what God, is like. He shows us the sort of heart the Father has. And what strikes us so wonderfully is that it is a vulnerable heart. A heart that can be wounded, that offers itself to us unprotected.

We see the Child absolutely dependent on the love and care of Mary and Joseph. Without them He would simply have died of cold, hunger, and sheer lovelessness.

I remember seeing in Cartmell Priory a huge, fibre-glass sculpture of the holy family on its flight into Egypt. Joseph is sitting on a low rock, having fallen asleep in utter exhaustion. Mary too is fast asleep. She is sitting on the ground leaning between Joseph's spread knees. Her own knees are bent and the Child, who no doubt had initially been cradled in her arms, has escaped from both them and His clothing, and leans stark naked over His mother's knees, looking around Him at the wonderful night with its blazing stars.

There is not the slightest trace of fear or suffering on His eager little face. At this stage of His life He was protected from life's bitterness by the love of these two. It is they who bear the cold and hunger, the fear and anxiety. It is they who must plot and plan to save the Child.

We can perhaps recall how much this idea meant to St Thérèse. She expressed it many times in a variety of ways. She had grasped that in some mysterious way God suffers from our sufferings, and she wanted to spare Him all she could. This made her careful to make little of her own trials and sadnesses. She refused to present them even to herself; she dismissed them as lightly as she could because she knew God would 'feel' for her. And then the image of herself as the Child's toy, and the wonderful, tender, selfless love behind it. He hadn't to bother with her – only find His pleasure in her when and as He wanted. She interpreted all that happened to her in this light. Everything that was saddening her – bitchiness in community, tiring, un-pleasant work, the cold, loneliness, her own dryness and inner sadness – all were accepted for His sake. She realised we can accept these things with love or else give way to anger, intolerance, complaint, lack of charity, retaliation, and thus wound the heart that has made itself so vulner-able.

Life is only for love. Thérèse knew this *practically*. She refused all desire for grandeur and just trained herself to recognise His calling, His demands, His love in the little events, both pleasant and unpleasant of daily life . . . trained herself not to miss a single opportunity. Oh, how different from us! It is because our Lord isn't a reality to us. Perhaps we haven't meditated sufficiently on Him, haven't lived with Him day in and day out. Perhaps we have lived too occupied with ourselves and so we don't know Him in such a way that everything without exception is seen in His light and responded to with love. We haven't grasped how our infidelities, our occupation with ourselves, our lack of charity to our neighbour, really hurts Him.

Perhaps when we reflect on the tender, human side of Jesus' birth, of His mother's careful shielding of Him, her ensuring that He did not suffer, we can see how we do exactly the same when we protect with anxious care our close union with Him.

True Contemplation

Mary is called the queen of contemplatives, the mistress of the interior life. But what does this mean? To live a contemplative life is to live at depth; to live below the surface in the world of faith, the world of reality and not appearances.

It is Luke who tells us that the mother of Jesus was the very epitome of holiness and the model of perfect discipleship. What we are told of her holiness is expressed basically in three sayings.

The first: 'I am the handmaid of the Lord, be it done to me according to your word.' I am yours absolutely. Do your will in me and through me I have no ambitions even of the most religious and spiritual kind. Do your will in darkness if needs be, in pain if needs be I do not ask to understand, I commit myself to you completely... This is the perfect contemplative stance.

The second glimpse into Mary comes through Elizabeth: 'Blessed are you for your believing, everything the Lord promised you will be fulfilled.' The culmination of God's promises is in you. You have allowed him to fulfil his will in you.

And in between this perfect offering of trust and its final consummation in her Assumption we are told that 'Mary kept all these words and pondered them in her heart.' Yes, blessed are they who hear the word of God and keep it.

We do not know how our Lady spent her days, the details are unimportant. We are told the only things that matter and which must be true of all who belong to Christ.

Contemplative living has writ large into it this Marian attitude or mode of being. We are to be contemplatives living in the depths of reality.

This sounds marvellously exciting and dramatic but it is just the opposite. Our fantasy can take us into excitements, delights, satisfactions. Faith keeps us in the here and now: in this moment and no other, in this situation and no other. Here is my Jesus, here in this moment, this duty, this set of circumstances. What a test of faith is this daily round, this pressure of seeming trivialities! What a test of faith in the dull, wearing pain, lacking all glamour and grandeur!

All the time, the heart of the contemplative is racing out beyond appearances, to embrace the Beloved who cannot be seen, cannot be felt. It means being drawn secretly to God away from reassuring limits and into his mysterious Self.

Mary's inner epic found expression in the martyrdom of her Son, but there is a sense in which the external form is unimportant.

The essentials for Mary were the three facets already out-lined – 'Your handmaid – do absolutely what you will' lived out in hearing the word of God and doing it; and at last the consummation of perfect faith and surrender – God's promises completely fulfilled.

Mary has allowed herself to be transformed by love into what she was called to be.

This is the end of contemplation.

Become as Little Children

There are many wonderful things to be contemplated in the actual childhood of Jesus but what I want to concentrate on is the *essence* of child: on that in Jesus which could always be called 'child' and which He summons all His disciples to become.

When Jesus takes a little child, puts him by His side and says 'Unless you become as little children you cannot enter the Kingdom of Heaven', what is He saying?

He is saying: 'Look at this child. There you have an image of my deepest truth which you too must live.'

The child is Jesus Himself. We are being told that, grown, strong, splendid, decisive man that He is, His deepest, most inward reality in His mortal life, is child. That is the mystery of the Child of Christmas. In His life there is no greater stature than childhood.

The words concerning the child are set in a context of a squabble for power and ascendancy, and also after Jesus' prediction of His coming passion. Essentially the same message could have been presented by the *Ecce Homo*, but this was too intolerable for His disciples. He used a softer image, one nearer to hand but hardly less scandalous.

What is Jesus speaking of? He is speaking of powerlessness, unimportance. It is foolish to put the weight on innocence, docility, etc. – children differ. He was speaking rather of something fundamental. Every child is powerless; he is unimportant (and knows it!) He doesn't manage the world, he doesn't rule his own life, he can only receive everything, for better or worse, from others. If he isn't provided for he can do nothing about it. He is completely dependent.

Jesus is saying that spiritually, in the world of God, we have to be just like that. We are not autonomous, we are in relationship. We are dependent on our Father – our Provider, our Security, our Lover. He must be obeyed, and that is terrible to our pride.

We want to be persons in our *own* right, taken account of, with control over our own destiny and that of the world. We are innately sensitive to our rights and prerogatives. We want to be somebody of ourselves. We want to achieve something.

In what matters most in life, says Jesus, you have to renounce this self with its urges, claims, rights, dignity. You have to willingly, lovingly, recognise that you are powerless and that everything you can do is unimportant. You are as dependent on Me for your well-being and spiritual growth as is the child on its parents.

How many are content to live out their mortal lives in union with Jesus in experienced poverty and helplessness? How many are content to be there just to receive, to let God be God? Truly we have to die and be born again as a little child.

Let us beg for this grace as we gaze on the Babe of Bethlehem.

Acceptance

Our Lord took to Himself the full burden of human help-lessness, and it was in it, through it, and from it that He loved and surrendered Himself to His Father. He never sought to escape from it nor did He accept the avenues of possible escape.

Michaelangelo shows us the spiritual quality of this acceptance, the inner, unseen reality of it.

Here is Mary, the most beautiful of women with her beautiful Son. She reminds us of a lioness in her magnificent poise and strength – a lioness with her perfect cub.

Strong, serene, she accepts what the future holds for her child. She can do this because she knows that God is Father. This unshakeable faith in the fatherhood of God is the counterpoint of human helplessness. We are happy to be helpless so that God can be God to us, and a God who is, of His very nature, Father.

Mary has said yes – 'Yes, I accept to be a woman and all

PITTI MADONNA *Michelangelo*

43

that means. I accept the suffering, the striving, the heart-rendings and detachments that must be if I am to become a woman. I willingly offer my Son to You in spite of the pain.'

Virgin and Mother

When we say Our Lady is Mother we mean that she is supremely life-giving. Wherever she is, whatever she touches, is awakened to life. Life flows out from her finger-tips. She is like a whirling ball of fire throwing off life-giving sparks. She is so filled with life herself that she cannot but overflow onto all who come within her orbit, and the life she radiates is always the life of Jesus.

She is mother, she is virgin. These terms are not, as often supposed, contradictory. Spiritually speaking you cannot have one without the other. You cannot be a true mother unless you are utterly virginal, and you cannot be truly virginal without being a mother.

What is spiritual virginity? It would be a mistake to confuse it with the physical state of virginity. Spiritual virginity belongs to the fullness of the Christian vocation and is for all, married or unmarried. Celibate consecration draws attention to it, symbolises it, but unless it is united to spiritual virginity it is worthless.

Spiritual virginity means being totally for God. It means loving God with the whole of oneself – with all the heart, all the soul, all the mind, all the strength. It means recognising in a practical way that God alone is one's fulfilment, and it means looking only to Him, be it in marriage or consecrated celibacy for that fulfilment.

For those of us called to a life of celibacy we can see that we have a special function in the church. We are to experience in the flesh the fact that we have no meaning, no fulfilment except in God. Like the virgin of the Old Testament we are poor, without a husband. Our womb is barren, our arms are empty. But Scripture shows us that it is precisely this shamed one, this poor one, the barren woman like Sarah or Hannah, who becomes the bearer of God's promise; and this reaches its culmination in Mary.

What we must note, however, is that we must bear with love this state of virginity – what we might call the desert state, with its inevitable pain. The pain must serve only to cast us more deeply into God in blind faith.

Let us beware of infidelity and the seeking of cheap compensations. Rather, let us, like Mary, find happiness in our nothingness, take pride in our state of empty longing, waiting in silent trust . . . utterly certain, not that one day He *will* come but that, here and now, He *comes*. Here and now He is filling my emptiness, causing my desert to blossom like the lily.

It is only in accepting to be truly virginal that we can flower in motherhood. To be virginal is to be fruitful. Any state of virginity that is not fruitful is a sham. Something has gone wrong. It is not spiritual virginity. The liturgy sings that Mary was virginal both before, during and after the birth of her Child. Below this all too human and masculine formulation lies, as nearly always, a jewel of truth preserved by the Holy Spirit. Before the Incarnation Mary was wholly virginal. According to her capacity she was living for God alone, looking solely to Him for fulfilment, waiting on Him.

This acceptance of virginity, this empty longing was answered. Her womb burgeoned, her arms were filled with her holy Child. Yet she was never allowed to sink into mere natural maternity. A sword pierced her heart from the outset, and her human motherhood of Jesus is shown to us in the Scriptures as full of pain and detachment. In this her inner virginity was only increased. And after His death, how deep her human loss and loneliness! Yet at the same time how profound her joy in her deep awareness of union with Him, and in her motherhood of John a premonition of what her motherhood was, and would be forever.

Personal Epiphany

No one seems to know what Rembrandt had in mind when he painted this mysterious rider. Perhaps, as with all great artists, he was expressing truth deeper than he could know.

It seems to me an image of what it means to go the whole way to God. I have seen His star in the east and must go to meet Him who comes. He is the God who comes, who is always coming, and we are always on the move, a pilgrim people, going out to meet Him, always leave-taking, journeying on from where we are to where we are not. To go to Him where He is must always mean a journey into seeming shadows, into what cannot be understood, is unknown, unfamiliar, and therefore frightening. To reach Him who is beyond our knowledge we must go by a way we do not know.

The rider's gaze is serene, gentle, abandoned; it is the horse who strains ahead with impassioned face as if he knows the way. The rider does not try to control him, rather he trusts himself to him, holding the reins loosely.

POLISH RIDER *Rembrandt*

This pathetic, scraggy beast, whose head alone is noble, is human life.

Human life, wholly lived, takes us surely to God, there is no other mount. The poverty of our human condition and life can 'scandalise' us, so ungoldy, so lacking in beauty and glory we are tempted to find another, nobler beast. None but this one can take us to God.

There is no moment, no happening however banal and seemingly Godless, but holds God for us, represents His summons to Himself. It is the surest guidance and we need no other light. This rider has turned his back on all that the world holds, all that is merely for self. He gazes into far horizons, looking for His Lord, eyes and heart only for Him. He is Jesus in his earthly life going resolutely on His way to His Father.

Child of Light

When his parents brought the Child Jesus into the temple, Simeon held out his arms to receive Him.

An old man stretches out for the Child, the Child comes to him like a bird to its nest.

Here is a picture of what can be, of what should be. He always comes to waiting arms.

Jesus comes as a light to us today. Let us ask Him for the courage and the desire to extricate ourselves from all that enmeshes us.

Let us ask Him to show us how our arms are kept back from stretching towards Him. Let us begin all over again to live for Him.

Simeon's selflessness is an echo of Jesus' selflessness. Simeon and Jesus suit one another. They fit together. They make one whole. Both have one mind, one will. This is what can be, what should be. This is what Christian life is all about.

Today we receive a candle, symbol of our Lord. A candle

T.W.I.H—C

is also put into our hands at Baptism, and again on Easter night, as we recall our Christian beginnings.

Let us receive it today with great faith. Let us beg Christ with our heart's strength to purify us, to enkindle a fire of love within us. We want our inner dispositions to fit the action.

And as a candle burns it consumes itself. So let us pray that as each day each year passes, everything is for Him, and our whole substance is spent for Him alone.

*Lent
and
Easter
Cycle*

Lenten Witness

Witness to my love in this way: obey my voice, stand in the gate and hear the word of the Lord.

Put oil on your heads, the oil of gladness, and wash your faces of all gloom.

Show one another that it is a privilege and a joy to be dedicated to the Father.

Resist every temptation to self pity. Not one complaint, not one grumble, even an interior one.

Make little of anything that hurts. Instead tell the Father how happy we are to have these little opportunities to show our love for Him.

If we obey this summons how happy we shall be! How profoundly we shall enter into Jesus' own self-giving! How deeply we shall live our Christian life!

And what an alms-giving this would be to a lost bewildered world.

Baptised in Christ

Baptism is a key word in Lent. As we know, its institution was as a period of intense preparation for baptism at the Easter Vigil, and ideally it still has this slant. Baptism is never over and done with. Baptism is a state – it must always continue. We have been put into a state of Baptism and we must live out the truth of that state.

What does it mean to be baptised? Various answers will come to mind, but if the answers are authentic they will reflect different aspects of the basic truth. Baptism is ultimately the sacrament of the Fatherhood of God, by it we become His sons and daughters, which is what human-hood is all about.

How is this metamorphosis of becoming a child of God effected? By dying to our purely natural life and being born again into new life, spiritual life, the life of the Risen Christ which is the life of God Himself.

Baptism takes us up into the movement of Jesus, 'I go to the Father.' We know the incredible pain, grief, darkness of that journey which we call the passion and death of Jesus. Basically it is *our* journey through the sadness and darkness sin or estrangement from God has caused. It is because our only way to the Father lies through death that Jesus died. He transformed that dark passage. Now it is truly a pathway of light leading straight to the Father.

We are summoned to faith. Summoned to deny, move off our own base and to stand on God's fidelity as revealed in Jesus. We are summoned to accept His judgements, His values, His point of view; to surrender to His will, His guidance. The opposite of sin is not virtue but faith. Faith destroys sin as light destroys darkness.

To be baptised, to live in the state of baptism is to live in and by faith: not just to make acts of faith now and then but to live our lives by faith – absolute trust in the forgiving, self-donating God.

What we tend to do is live faith in fits and starts, acknowledging Him in some areas, denying Him in others. Baptism only becomes total when faith is total. Then truly we have died with Christ to a purely human life, and risen to His divine way of being.

There can be no realism in our living unless we keep our eyes on the blessed passion of Christ, and Lent is the time when the Church bids us accept the pain of having this sacred passion always before our eyes. In the passion we measure the greatness of His love, the seriousness of our lives with their countless choices, the certitudes upon which we base ourselves.

Lent is the time of effort, warfare, discipline. Let us look and look again at the suffering Jesus and take the weight of shame and sorrow.

It is often said, and rightly, that we cannot contemplate the death and resurrection of Jesus save in the radiance of the resurrection. But because of what we are, there is a need that, at a particular time of year we should, as it were, step

out of this radiance and stand in the unredeemed dark –
looking at what our sins have done, looking at what our
redemption cost the Lord.

'You who have been baptised in Christ are clothed head
to foot in Christ.' Let us accept the shame of the necessary
stripping so that we may indeed rise anew at Easter, clothed
in the glory of the Risen Jesus.

Fire on Earth

'I have come to enkindle a fire on earth.'

A little investigation, if I am not mistaken, reveals that the fire of the sun is the motor force of this planet. Fire is energy both for life more abundant and life more destructive. Earth is vibrating continually under the influence of fire: fire at times so delicate, giving colour to flower petals and butterflies' wings, at times so devastating . . . burning up forests and mountains.

But there is another fire of which natural fire is only the symbol. This is the fire Jesus speaks of – the fire of Divine Love.

We live in the modern world, and how perilous a world it seems. Man has found the secret of energy. He has entered into the holy place and snatched away the secret of fire. Who can predict the outcome? This discovery has shaken the world to its foundations. Press a button and there is inconceivable destruction.

Appalling knowledge and power are in the hands of man.

59

He has, we say, come of age, and in a sense this is true. It would be wrong of us, I am convinced, to look out upon the world and see only evil and sin. Good is circulating every bit as much as evil, and more so.

We tend to measure sin and evil by observable effects. True, there are some human acts which bring immediate, shameful, painful or shattering results, and readily we exclaim 'What a terrible sin!' But pure mistake and bungling can bring exactly the same results.

It happens similarly in our own lives. Often we feel more upset and sorry about something that was only a mistake but which wrought observable harm, or something that others have witnessed and condemned, than we do about serious matters that lack these outward signs. And yet, in the deepest spiritual order, they are infinitely more harmful.

I suspect that many of the things which, to our limited point of view appear drastically sinful, are not so in God's eyes. Can we think otherwise than that basically man's struggle to uncover the secrets of nature, to harness its power, is glorious for God? Surely it is; but such enterprises inevitably involve enormous risks and dangers. God wants His children to grow up, wants them to shake off ignorance, to forswear magic and superstition. The mistakes and calamities which follow may well fall within His loving providence. *We* find them ghastly but that does not prove that He does.

Alas! we have to recognise that our spiritual growing up does not keep pace with our growth in knowledge and the power knowledge gives. We are made more aware of the awful effects of selfishness. In times past the majority of men and women lacked power to inflict damage on a large scale. To kill another, one had to be near him. Now he can be killed from thousands of miles away. But we cannot argue from that that the inner selfishness is any greater.

What has to be faced is that growth in knowledge and power demands growth in responsibility – and this demands selflessness.

The basis of all sin is egocentricity. Instead of a fire of love burning in the heart there is a fire of self-centredness. To combat evil in the world we must begin with our own hearts. Each of us must learn to love. Human maturity means the ability to love, to be outside oneself, free to devote oneself to love. This is never natural; it can be gained only through the grace of God and immense personal effort.

If we are people of real prayer we know that the same evil which could potentially destroy the world is within our own hearts. We are as much the perpetrators of what we see or think to be crime as those who put their hand, their signature to it. Each must do what he or she can to counteract the evils in society, each according to their own vocation, but that is not enough. We should be quick to recognise every exercise of selfishness in our day to day lives.

There is absolutely no difference in destructive power between a seemingly small act of selfishness on my part and what the world can actually see and experience as destructive. My selfishness destroys life and love on a world scale.

Prayer should keep us exposed to the Fire which will reveal all our impurities and give us no rest; and, if we will, it will gradually transform us so that we too become fire – the most powerful force on earth.

If only we would bring to our hidden surrender the same energy, the same dedication, which men and women all over the world bring to their public protest and campaigning!

Obedience

We speak of Jesus' sinlessness, but if we look carefully at the letters of St Paul we see that for him the chief characteristic of Jesus' life, the characteristic which *showed* his sinlessness was His obedience.

Obedience means having an open ear and a listening heart, like Jesus never, ever, saying 'No' or even a partial 'No'.

New Testament writers do not allow us to think of Jesus as living a protected life, free from the batterings and assaults that fall to our lot in a sinful world. Rather, he *learned* obedience from what He underwent. Jesus recognised more and more his Father's will in the world around Him. And as He recognised Him so He surrendered in increasing love; not without struggle, not without groans, tears and ultimately a sweat of blood – a 'Yes' that cost every ounce.

This obedience of Jesus, this perfect response is the world's salvation.

Evil in the true sense is Adam's (everyman's) disobedience, his 'Nos' and 'half-Nos'. Jesus' perfect obedience puts things right again. He is our representative; He does it for us – but not instead of us! It isn't a case of, He died so we don't have to. No, He died so that we can die that death which is true life. He obeyed perfectly so that we too can obey perfectly. With and through Jesus we can overcome the world's evil.

Eyes on the Lord

This virgin martyr rests on the instrument of her martyr-dom – an appallingly cruel instrument, a wheel of knives to which she is tied and cut to pieces. Yet she stands, a magnificently womanly woman, with her gaze serenely fixed on God. She is a woman of faith, looking beyond appearances, beyond the way in which He comes to Him who comes.

Now we are tied to the wheel of life – a slower process, less cruel, but more prolonged. How do we see it? How do we take it? Like Catherine? As hour by hour something is demanded of me, opportunities for letting go of self for the sake of others, to be faithful to my duties, do I always let go, entrust myself to life (which is really to Him), or do I allow my egotism to evade the demands – perhaps wholly, perhaps in part?

When life presses, when I am attacked by a mood of depression, boredom, frustration, self-pity, do I give in to it and remain absorbed in self? Or do I, like Catherine, fix my

ST CATHERINE OF ALEXANDRIA Raphael

eyes on Him and see that this is precisely what takes me to Him, this is how He comes.

Monotony, other people with their irritating characteristics which get on my nerves, the daily, inexorable round of duties material and spiritual . . . all these form the wheel on which I go to Him. Only insofar as I really accept life and refuse to evade will I become a real woman, as distinct from being just a female of the human species.

A woman takes life, lives life. She learns to love no matter what the cost to herself; she forgets herself for love. A woman lives by principles, not by her ever changing feelings – and for a Christian, principles are simply the teachings of Jesus or the will of God.

If we really let go and surrender, then what we find so irksome naturally speaking becomes precious to us – we can lean on it, cease to fear it. We grasp that it is really Jesus Himself.

Old Age

Old age is part of human life, a part Jesus Himself did not share. Nevertheless, He bore all our infirmities, carried all our sorrows.

The infirmities of old age link us very closely to Jesus if we accept them with humility. To do this we need to look constantly at our Saviour in His suffering, His love and His patience. The disabilities of old age and sickness seem to make us less human – 'without beauty, without majesty', and yet, in the eyes of the Father we are infinitely beautiful just as we are.

When we think deeply about it, all our infirmities of body and mind are an expression of our need for God. Our very body witnesses to the fact that we are unfulfilled, incomplete. When we feel the weight of it all we can turn that weight into a cry for God. 'My soul is thirsting for God, the God of my life.'

Old age plays a vital role in God's plan. If we were cut off in youth or in middle life most of us would still be full of selfishness, we should be unpurified, unformed. In His mercy God gives us old age when we are forced to detachments we were not generous enough to make freely.

So much has to go in old age, we lose one thing after another. But everything depends on how we accept this knife of detachment when God prunes His vine to make it bear abundant fruit.

Old age, well received, is a wonderful opportunity for repairing lost chances. As we grow older and feel the weight of years let us put ourselves totally into the hands of the Divine vine-dresser, that He may accomplish in us all that we promised to give Him in our youth.

Always Confident

'Holiness does not consist in this or that practice but rather in a disposition of the heart that makes us always humble and little in the arms of God, well aware of our frailty but boldly confident in his Fatherly goodness.' (THÉRÈSE OF LISIEUX)

To say that these words of Thérèse are significant is an understatement, they are in fact momentous. St Thérèse here gives us the key to the whole mystical life, and one which admirably suits our modern age. Hers was a path devoid of extraordinary graces. It was a way simply of the theological virtues and the gifts of the Holy Spirit. She demonstrates that these, and nothing else, embody the essence of holiness, and that these are pure gift. Holiness is all gift, 'all is grace'; in what then can we boast?

It seems there are only two things we can give God: trust and acceptance of poverty.

Confidence, not love, is basic. Love is the summit, and

confidence leads to love. I am sure it is confidence we need to develop and pay most attention to; all the rest will flow from it. We have to take God at his word, 'Ask and you will receive, seek and you shall find.'

We really have to believe that God wants to give us nothing less than Himself, is only waiting to pour Himself into us. We have to take Him at His word as He reveals Himself in the Gospels – the friend of sinners, one who throws His arms around the wayward, ungrateful son and kisses him in all his filthy rags. This is God.

Does our disposition of soul respond to this God or have we formed our own image of Him projected from human experience? The biggest obstacle to trust seems to be a wrong idea of God, a projection of our self-image. We feel unlovable therefore God cannot love us, or so we think. By faith we know this is nonsense, but the feeling obstinately persists and can stifle and overwhelm us.

How can we tackle this feeling of worthlessness, for it is not on the rational but on the emotional level? First, I think we have to recognise that we cannot get rid of it by sheer willing. All the meditations in the world won't shake it off. Therefore it must be accepted. I have to accept its falsity and pain and then act against it – talk to God about it. When downcast at some revelation of misery, when I feel I haven't even begun in the spiritual life, when I see myself the prey to evil inclinations, tempted to anger, bitterness, resentment, jealousy . . . when I am helpless, distracted at prayer, feeling completely unlovable . . . *then* is the moment for glorious confidence.

We must trust God enough to know that He would never leave us in a state of weakness without a purpose. He wants us to glorify Him in it. It is at moments like these, when we feel utterly disgusted with ourselves, that we must turn to God with all our heart.

If only we had Thérèse's insight here! She saw the grace

of these bitter moments and declared them hours of joy. She prayed to God to give her an ever clearer insight into her weakness. 'Where shall we find one who is truly poor in spirit?' she cries. This acceptance of self, this joyful realisation of being always weak, always imperfect, is the greatest gift we can give to God. When He sees that humility is our way of being, when we have chewed on, masticated our nothingness, when we know experimentally that without Him we can do nothing, then He may hand us virtues – patience, fortitude, meekness, love, prayer.

It is far more important to God that we have this disposition of heart, this awareness of our nothingness, than that we should attain to sublime heights, prove to ourselves and others how holy we are, how patient, how meek, how charitable. All He asks is our goodwill. If we fail *He* is not offended, so why should *we* be upset?

The feature of God's intervention is our peaceful acceptance of our imperfection. We come to accept ourselves as we are and reality as it is. We accept our life, destiny, circumstances, other people, and we accept because we trust. God in secret is infusing knowledge of Himself as love.

Finally God takes over completely. We pass from our own hands into His. Our dark, confident contemplation, has borne the fruit of union.

The Cross and the Crucified

The Cross stands on the rim of the world dominating the cosmos. The Crucified gives meaning to the cosmos: the Crucified and the man who has chosen to cleave to the Cross – the true contemplative.

Tenderness has left an indelible trace on the face of the dead Jesus inclining towards the man kneeling at His feet. It is the tenderness of God Himself enfolding all that He has made. 'How can anything be amiss? And all shall be well and all manner of things shall be well.' (*Revelations of Divine Love*, by Julian of Norwich.)

Dominic is so close to the Cross that he cannot see the tenderness of the glance directed to him. He doesn't *see* it, but he believes it, knows it. And so he just keeps on quietly faithful, loyal, loving, not occupied with himself but only with Jesus. Grave, unselfish, absorbed – a true contemplative entering deeply into the saving work of Jesus.

DOMINIC AT THE FOOT OF THE CROSS   *Fra Angelico*

Precious to God

If we attend to the passion of Christ we hear a voice insisting 'Someone died for you.' And of that someone dying it can with all truth be said that God is there, bearing the burden of our wrongdoing, the burden of our pain, loneliness and death. God is there loving us totally, holding back nothing. And because He died for us and lived for us, our lives in all their trivialities, their joys and burdens, have meaning in Him. They hold Him within them, through them we can surrender to Him.

How precious we must be to God! How momentous our life span! Yet we value ourselves so lightly, waste the precious content of our being, never reach fulfilment. We do not really live but allow life to pass us by.

God wants us to seize hold of life, hoard its unique opportunities for growth, grasp its chances to express our love and gratitude to Him who loved us first.

Every moment of our life can be filled with eternity, because at every moment, in every event and circumstance we can say our 'Yes' to God who wills us to live to capacity, wills us to act as full persons.

How many of us act from our inmost centre according to principles, not merely following the crowd, the line of least resistance, seeking immediate satisfactions and appreciation? Meanwhile the days and years pass by and we remain essentially undeveloped.

Yet Someone died for us that we might live with abundant life.

Do Not Judge

Let us dwell for a while on that particular sin which our Lord emphasises specially – the sin of judging others.

The human heart is God's secret, we simply cannot know it; yet how readily we make judgements and impute motives. We feel absolutely sure of things, we get upset or feel angry, we fall into lots of other sins because we have allowed ourselves to judge.

No matter how obvious it seems to us, remember we simply cannot know another's motivations. All we are saying in fact is that if *I* did such and such it would be for these reasons, therefore these reasons must be hers too.

The hidden sin of judging, so common, so little regarded, is a tremendous obstacle to God's love. Because it is secret, because it seems such a natural thing to do, because we feel we see things aright, we have no contrition, our consciences remain untroubled. Whereas a thing of less moral significance which is obvious to ourselves and others can rack us with guilt feelings which we mistake for real sorrow.

Contrition means 'never again.' 'With all my heart I renounce this habit. I will examine myself on it daily . . . honestly, ruthlessly . . .'

> Plenteous grace with thee is found
> Grace to cleanse from every sin.
> Let the healing streams abound.
> Make and keep me pure within.
>   (From *Jesu lover of my soul* v. 4. Charles Wesley)

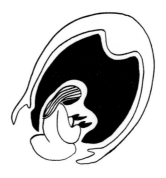

The Gift of Ourselves

St Thérèse saw the infinite love of God as a pent up ocean, yearning and aching to release its torrents which are held back by our barricades. If we remove the barricades these waters of love flow over us carrying all before them. Thérèse longed to be one who would give God the joy of being able to love her fully, to give full vent to His love. Shall we not desire this also?

'I have come to cast fire on the earth and how I yearn for it to be kindled.' I seek an earth dried and parched with longing, free from the cloying moisture of self love. One touch of fire to such a heart and there is a conflagration. An earth seeping with self love cannot be ignited.

Recall the water Elijah poured on the earth and how this was consumed by flames (cf. 1 Kings 18: 35).

So we can water our earth with contrition, and this too can become a conflagration. It is never too late to give ourselves entirely to God. We waste time on self reproach

and discouragement, when we should be throwing ourselves into God's arms.

May He *today* be able to rejoice: I came, and at last she
could receive me. Now I can make her happy, now I can fill
her with myself.

The Way of the Cross

The picture reproduced over the page is an attempt to put the way of the Cross where it truly belongs – in contemporary human life. Breughel has set it right in his own context and he hasn't 'minced his words' as we would say.

This haphazard crowd is representative of the common man flocking to and around the execution ground where there is always something interesting to see: besides, it's central to the life of the little town with much coming and going. Some folks are just about their business as usual, and this procession has only a nuisance value. Others are curious, others just enjoy the excitement, and the children seem to be finding it an opportunity for fun.

There is cruelty, callousness, frivolity, naive crude sympathy; and some deeper emotions in those most intimately connected with the condemned. At the centre of the picture is a small, insignificant figure fallen beneath His cross. Save for a few, He is arousing no more nor less interest than the many criminals who have passed this way to the gibbet-

strewn common. Two others likewise condemned are preceding Him. They look with fearful eyes at the gibbets
round which the birds of prey are hovering.

Truly a terrible scene of what man is; and it gives us a
little idea of what it means to say God became man, shared
our life and died our death. There was nothing romantic
about it, only sordid, painful reality.

Jesus' mother and friends are helpless to help Him; they
cannot get near Him. How well this portrays the grief of
millions who have seen their loved ones tortured and killed.

We must pray that the great human scene be lit up for us
and given meaning by Jesus. Somehow, seeing Jesus bearing His cross in the midst of everything, this picture is
robbed of its meaningless horror. We understand that this is
the world God loves, and He takes on Himself our terrible
human sin and misery – so that we may have life – and have
it abundantly.

THE WAY OF THE CROSS *Breughel*

Beata Passio

On Palm Sunday we reach the quayside. A great ship is fretting at the moorings, sail unfurling in the bright sunshine; a beautiful ship with the line and grace of a bird. A cry goes out from it: 'All on board!' and eager hands reach out to help us onto the deck; the hands of those who have made the journey before us and whose home is in the land to which we are invited.

This great ship of Holy Week will carry us surely, strongly, into the Passion of Christ, the blessed Passion of Christ as our fathers' insight named it. On the prow is blazoned the name 'Love's Victory'. All we have to do now is board the ship and allow it to take us all the way. We have nothing else to do but let it take us. We have not to do the navigating ourselves, we have not to labour with the oars, we have not to see where we are going or what distance we are covering: all that is being done for us. We have only to say 'Let it be done. Give me all you want to give. Be my Saviour, be my God'.

The time of strife and warfare is over. The weeks of Lent were for that. The time of looking at ourselves and our shortcomings is past, the time even of reflection on what our sins have cost him. These are the exercises which bring us to the quayside, but from now on we forget ourselves and look only at Him. Look – not in the sense that I try to meditate on his physical sufferings, try to bring home to myself the enormity of His pain, try to identify with that; but in the sense that I remain in His heart, allow myself to be taken into what is the essence of Jesus and the essence of His Passion and death – His giving all, absolutely all to His Father.

Three o'clock on Good Friday: that moment symbolises for us the hour of His glorification. The young Prince of Glory dies with a cry of humble pride, 'It is consummated'. (It is quite, quite finished! Nothing remains that is not given. Oh, I have given everything, everything! What joy, supreme human joy to have given God everything from childhood on, in joy and pain, in fear, doubt and grief, in temptation, in obscurity, in seeming godlessness, in the nightmare of horror, degradation and agony in which I have been caught up. I give my last, I *choose* to die, to cast myself over into nothingness certain that there are my Father's arms. Into your hands Father I cast myself. And lo, I am with you. The darkness is past, no darkness at all, only the light of your lovely Face. Your gentle hands which had seemed so harsh – but I always knew they were all love – are holding me and filling me with joy. The mystery in which I have lived and loved and never doubted or swerved from embracing is now luminous to me. I have passed through the valley of death, the dark and terrible valley, and lo, I am with you still. I have always been with you for you have always been with me. You have never left me alone, but I have *felt* alone and abandoned. Now I see you, now I feel you, FATHER. Now I know what it means, that word

Father. Now I savour throughout my being what it is to be your Son. And now, O joy of joys! I bring my brethren with me. They too come through the dark valley made a place of springs. I have done it all for them: slain the beast, marked the path so surely. They do not go through alone for I am always with them. The victory is certain. Alleluia!)

If we want a focus for our thoughts, think of the moment of Jesus' death and long to share it. There is nothing to debar you. Look more at His heart than at his physical sufferings. The only value of these is what His love gave them. He would not want us to spend much time and energy on them.

We join the disciples on Palm Sunday staying close to Him, watching Him, listening to His words to know His soul: John the Evangelist tells us that it was precisely when Jesus saw the crowd approaching from the city in a frivolous, messianic mood, that He took a donkey and sat on it, clearly showing that their expectations were quite false. 'In lowly pomp ride on to die.' By this time too Jesus is in *His* ship. He realises that His own efforts have failed and that He can do no more. The answer now lies with His Father. Everything seems hopeless, He a failed and doomed man, but His Father can be trusted to achieve His work in His own way.

Jesus now abandons Himself to events. Seeing the city He weeps over it. The city spread out before Him – the holy city representing the world God so dearly loves. Jesus who knows the Father's heart weeps His tears for Him. He goes on loving ungrateful, frivolous, hateful men: 'If only you would recognise even now what is for your blessed peace, but alas – you don't want to!' His mission is over. When approached by the Greeks He does not even see them. His Father will do it. Yes, they will come to know Him, the whole world will come to know Him, but only when the grain of wheat has died.

'With desire I have desired to eat this Pasch with you before I suffer.' This gives the key to His heart on Thursday. Each evangelist in his own way has created the same atmosphere of loving intimacy and joy, exultation almost, that the sense of impending disaster cannot overcome. Clearly Jesus knows this is the hour, the hour so long awaited, when His Father is to act and change the world. He knows too that He must die, that it is through His own sacrifice that God's great work of redemption will be done – how He does not know. What does His death matter, what matter the pain and fear compared with the glory to be gained? Having joy set before Him, the joy of saying 'Yes' to the Father, the joy of knowing that the whole world will be caught up in that surrender of love, He would endure whatever death awaited Him.

For the moment though, the thought of death is ghostly compared with the glorious expectation. Gladly He can give the memorial of His sacrifice, thus pledging Himself irrevocably to it – what we are to call the Sacrament of His Love. The Kingdom of God is coming, coming soon. Soon He will be drinking a wine wholly new in a wholly new world.

John the Evangelist in his last discourse gives us an idea of what was passing secretly in the depths of Jesus at this time . . .

Then He leaves the warm glow of the supper room to go out into the night, and suddenly it grips Him, a sense of just what death must mean. Gone the joyful expectancy, gone the gloriously experienced hope that made death seem trifling. How true to our human condition this is! He must struggle with it all, struggle with the nightmarish fear and growing horror. But His will never wavers. Each new challenge is met with a deeper 'Yes, even this.' Did He expect the assassin's dagger – from whence would it come? Or the violent mob which would summarily dispatch Him by stoning or throwing Him over a cliff? When would it strike? 'Oh, stay here, don't leave me alone!'

Could He have forseen the particularly awful nature of the death to which He was condemned? What when He saw how things were going, that He was being handed over to the Romans and what that might mean? How He would have to renew and renew in ever stronger movements the surrender He had always made!

Then He is caught up in the whirlwind of agony unabated. This is His hour of glory, His hour of purest love, when everything is outpoured, when His 'Amen' reaches its climax. This total self-emptying has an automatic counterpart, so to speak – He is fulfilled by the Father in His resurrection, glorification, ascension. It is consummated.

On Holy Saturday we have time to reflect quietly on this surrender of Jesus, to enter into it, 'hangs my helpless soul on Thee,') steeping ourselves in the joy of Jesus at the moment of His death, the moment of perfect trust and affirmation of the Father. A mysterious day. We know it has happened yet it is as if it had not – silence, non-event, like our life on earth. We live with this until Easter night when we look at the other side. That which eye hath not seen nor ear heard, nor the mind of man conceived, has become our dwelling place. We are home.

Let us then board the ship full of humble gratitude and trust. 'But I have not got to the quayside even. It seems to me I have wasted Lent wrapped up in myself.' Never mind. Here you are, brought by the community of the Church. Get on board. Don't waste further time in useless lamentations which give no joy to God. Get on board. The moorings are cast, the sails billow in the breeze, and we are carried off deep into the mystery of Jesus.

Pietà

Let us consider Mary as she cradles the dead Jesus after His crucifixion. Why does she in this role express irresistibly perfect love? It is because she has chosen Him in His passion and death, when He is utterly without beauty or attraction; when rather He is loathsome, He is dead, silent, there is not a vestige of response, she is getting nothing out of it save the pure joy of loving and being only for Him. She has entered into His passion.

Is it only now that she begins to understand? begins to see Him as He really is, and move into that reality which is dark, suffering mystery? 'When I am lifted up from the earth then I will draw all men to myself . . . in that day you will *know* . . .' and surely Mary above all – who was utterly faithful when she did not understand.

There is a deeper truth in Thomas' words than is immediately obvious. Unless I see the wounds in His hands and put my fingers in them, see the wound in His side and enter in, I simply *cannot* know Him, *cannot* believe in Him.

To become 'without beauty, without majesty,' is the price of union with Jesus in His death. Whilst we want anything at all for ourselves we cannot be wholly His.

What does it mean to share the death of Jesus? What is the cross of Christ? Is it physical suffering, mental anguish? No, these of themselves are not the cross of Jesus, these come to all men regardless of their distance or closeness to Him. Of themselves they do not bring us to Him; it is what we do with them that matters. Patiently borne in union with Jesus they open us to the cross of Christ.

To enter into the mystery of the cross, to really die with Jesus, is a mystical grace pure and simple. Nothing we can do brings it about nor allows us to know what it is. But we are invited to take up our own cross and follow Jesus, and this is the way to mystical union.

Thus everything in our lives becomes part of the cross we must shoulder. The generosity and love with which we do this is all important. Crucial to our growth is the readiness to embrace Jesus as *He* comes to us, not as *we* want Him, and nearly always He comes in the humiliation of His passion.

To make this a reality in our lives means making up our minds to embrace sacrifice. You know how St Thérèse speaks so often of her daily resolve not to let a single sacrifice pass ... feeling that a day without sacrifice was wasted. She was not making a cult of suffering, but she was determined not to miss Jesus when He came to her in the guise of what was painful or humiliating. Like Mary, she made a specific and constantly renewed choice to embrace Him in His ugliness – which they saw for what it was, the shining beauty of divine love.

We cannot live with this holy Face, without beauty, without attractiveness, unless we are willing to become like that too. But how often we stay with Him only to some extent and then turn away our eyes.

Can you imagine if we were to say to Mary: 'Are you suffering, Mary? Are you disappointed with what life has given you? Do you feel fulfilled? Do you feel you have achieved something? Would you have things different?' She would drag her sad eyes away from the Jesus who absorbs her and they would be without comprehension. 'What do you mean? *He* is Life, Love. I have no life of my own.' She is completely lost in Him.

This is what it should mean to be a contemplative.

Holiness

This is a picture of holiness. Holiness is love, and this is what love does. Love blots out the ego. Love is happy to have no face, no importance; Love desires nothing save to hold Jesus. It wants nothing for itself; it wants to be lost in Him, absorbed in Him. Only Jesus matters.

But the same thing has happened to Jesus Himself. His intense love for us has blurred, has killed Him. In death his head bends lovingly to the one who has lost herself in Him.

The dominant figure in this group, the peak of the pyramid is, in fact, he who is least important – Nicodemus. He was not a true follower, but because in the end he came forward, God gave him this dignity. But he has nothing of the significance of the blurred, fainting, almost ugly figures of Jesus and Mary – the 'lost' ones.

FLORENTINE PIETÀ WITH NICODEMUS   *Michelangelo*

I Am the Resurrection

In John's Gospel we see Jesus declaring Himself to be the Resurrection and the Life, not *after* His own resurrection but before it – at the very tomb of death, the tomb of Lazarus.

We see Jesus under the stress of deep emotion; an inner turmoil and conflict are struggling to find expression. He shudders and groans – why? Surely it is at the awfulness of death, at man's dull acceptance of it coupled with his lack of insight in its regard. Only Jesus is capable of seeing death as it is. Here He confronts it nakedly in the stinking corpse of His friend, in the grief of mourners under which the earth has ever groaned.

Jesus knows that He too must die; He too must cause terrible mourning. Yet from the depths of this bewilderment and frustration, under the weight of weakness, He declares that He Himself is the answer. 'I am Resurrection. I am Life. I end death, I am the death of death.' What an act of faith in the Father!

The Epistle to the Hebrews calls Jesus the pioneer of our salvation, He who leads us in our faith and brings it to perfection. He tasted death and tasted it once – for *all*.

Only He could *really* taste death because of His sinlessness, because of His knowledge of the Father and love for mankind. He knew the separation from God, the abyss which death epitomises. He had no Risen Jesus in which to hope. He had to go into the jaws of death totally alone with no guarantees, no sure knowledge of what 'risen life' was. He had nothing except His trust in the Father as Father. He descended into the abyss, into hell, and annulled it forever.

Death is still experienced by us as death on the intellectual and emotional level, but in reality the chasm is bridged. We have only to believe in Jesus, allow ourselves to be taken up in Him and carried across. We can never taste death, never see death, for, as He says, He has destroyed real death. He died once for all. No one can know that sort of death again unless they deliberately choose to do so.

Let us think of the faith of our pioneer who leads us foward. Reason and senses cried out in outrage against His fate. On the cross He voiced His dereliction; but He never wavered in His trust in the Father.

Our faith now is in the Risen Lord. Our reason and senses may search in vain for *proof* that all is different, that Divine Love enfolds us, that death in all its forms – sickness, pain, frustration, disappointment, loneliness, is not an evil but the very path to glory. Nothing can separate us from the love of the Risen Christ who is transforming the world.

We must affirm our faith over and over again, longing to be drawn more completely away from our sinful selves into His world, His existence. We must yearn to 'die' here to all that is not God, so that, truly living by His life, we may reveal Him to the world.

95

My Body – Given for You

The Mass is the very centre, the pulse of our faith. It puts us continually in the presence of our redemption, exposes us to it without mercy, if only we wish it so. Although most certainly every time this sacred rite is performed the mystery of our own redemption is renewed, still it is only so *for us* in the measure that our gifts are really there, that our inwardness conforms to the symbolic action of offering.

The Eucharist is the most sacred act of our day; the memorial of the Lord's death and resurrection, a sacrament of love, a sign of unity, a banquet where joyfully we partake of the living Bread come down from heaven, and drink the chalice of His Blood.

We are thus bathed in the new light of the Incarnate Word. His light, the light of faith, shines in our hearts, and must shine forth in our lives. As with Jesus, every thought, every action, every word must shine with the light of godhead, be a revelation of who the Father is.

The Mass is the source whence daily we draw the light, the strength, to live and love in this way.

Risen and Glorious

In Jesus we see the total actualisation of human reality, which consists in the fact that man is truly himself only when delivered up to God. In Jesus, human nature is so taken up by God, so possessed by God, as to be God's own reality.

Now look at the earthly existence of Jesus – a human history in a fallen world. His whole life was a revelation of who He is, the Son. In Him is perfect obedience and surrender: 'He who sees me sees the Father.' But we failed to see Him, failed to see the glory of the Only Begotten, until it was placarded on the cross. 'And I, if I am lifted up from the world will draw all things to myself.'

We do not see Jesus, the Son of the Father, until the grain of wheat has died, until He is lifted up. This is the hour of His glorification, when He shows Himself as the Son He is, delivered up to His Father in perfect surrender. 'Father, I place my soul in your loving hands.'

The Son's prayer is expressive of His way of being. This

is the handing over of the bodily man to the mystery of a loving, merciful God in the only way possible in a fallen world, in death.

In the same movement in which the Son delivers Himself, dedicates Himself, sacrifices Himself, the Father receives, transfigures and glorifies Him.

Thus many concepts which have for us a negative ring, are seen to be in a process of transfiguration. To realise our being we have to become a sacrifice with Jesus, a son in the Son. A sacrifice is a being that is not only offered but accepted, that has entered into the sphere of the divine. Self-renunciation, poverty, abandonment, dying to self, are simply movements towards God, in them we actualise our humanness and transcendance.

The offering, in no matter how small a degree, never takes place without a corresponding acceptance, a passing over into God. This is the mystery of death and resurrection, our share in the Paschal mystery of Christ. It goes on hour by hour, day by day. It can be completed only in actual physical death, then self-donation will be total.

In this context we can grasp that the experience of poverty, helplessness, and other painful things are really glory in disguise.

In Jesus we have everything. Let us trust Him to bring us to that fulfilment for which we long, knowing that even as we die, resurrection is burgeoning in our barren hearts.

Peace is My Gift

'Peace is my parting gift to you, my own peace, such as the world cannot give.'

We live in a world, as Jesus did, where nothing is reliable or stable; where nothing satisfies for long; where human beings are largely helpless and seemingly without meaning – spending a few years on this planet then disappearing for good, vanishing like the flower of the field. It is a world where terrible things can happen.

Someone is speaking to us out of this very world, One who knows the world by sheer experience, who is part of the world and who Himself is about to undergo the worst it can inflict.

Yes, I am going to the Father – supreme joyful news. Dry your tears forever Mary, I go to the Father who is infinitely great, who receives my trembling finitude into His everlasting embrace. I am telling you now so that when so awful a thing happens you may know its meaning and find peace – my own peace, my own joy. I leave you a peace so different

T.W.I.H—E

from the makebelieve peace the world gives.

My peace is based on absolute Reality that is total, accepting Love. You must be with me where I am, in the Father, in His beautiful, ineffable world. This is where you belong now; having got there myself I come to take you with me. My going is my coming – my Resurrection. I am here with you to the end of time. You can choose to live in a world where the prince of darkness rules, or live in the world of my Father. Choose to live in the Father's world with me or live in the world which knows Him not.

Mostly we prevaricate. In some ways, at some times, we are living in the Father's world, the world of the Risen Jesus; at other times we live in the world of non-faith. We do not really believe that Jesus is risen. We give intellectual and verbal consent to the fact, but we do not live every moment of our lives in accordance with that truth. We judge things from a merely human standpoint, as they strike the senses and our human estimation. We fail to hold everything against the bright backdrop of faith. Instead we allow our emotions to dictate to us what is real and what is not. Far too easily we give way to our moods, our fears, our uneasy feelings.

Set your troubled hearts at rest, banish your fears. Do you love me? Then what do your ups and downs matter? I am risen and with my Father, All is unutterably well, and well forever Dry your tears forever Mary. Choose. Live with me in the sunshine world of my Father or opt to live in your own subjective estimation of reality.

Let us not be mistaken. We are not talking about a state of emotional tranquillity which nothing can disturb. We are not speaking of emotion but of faith. We must act out our faith at every moment.

Notice how often Jesus tells us what love consists in: it consists in doing what He has commanded, doing always what pleases the Father. Note, *always*, not just now and then when we fell alright. There must be no identifying love of God with intense *feelings* of love, with sublime intellectual insight. Hence there must be no anxiety, no discouragement when spiritually we feel dull and drab.

To say Jesus is risen is to say He has come back to us. This is our joy, our certainty, the security in which we live out our days.

He is with us, not in limitation but with the whole weight of His Father behind Him. He comes in the Father, with the Father. He brings the Father to us as He promised: 'We shall come to him and make our abode in him.' So up, let us go forward to do the will of that same Father.

Transfigured in Christ[1]

Here is a woman who truly symbolises the consecrated soul. She is totally present to what she is doing. Her work is accomplished with the recollection, the dedication, of Mary; but like Martha she serves others too from her solitude.

The broken bread, the poured liquid, mirror her own life of profound self-giving. Even the way she stands shows something of her inner dignity. She is irradiated with light, the light of Jesus.

In this light her very flesh is transformed, so that she becomes a living sign of the Risen One, accomplishing her tasks as He accomplished His Father's will.

He lives again in the one who is truly given; the one who allows herself to live in His light, and to be made golden by the Sun of Love.

[1] This meditation is by Elizabeth Ruth Obbard.

THE MILKMAID *Vermeer*

True Joy

Christian joy is no mere emotion even though it may, and often does overflow into our emotional and sensitive experience. Christian joy is a virtue, that is, a power of the soul: it is a fruit of the Holy Spirit of God who dwells within us. It is a sharing in the very joy of Jesus. 'I have spoken thus to you, that my joy may be in you and your joy may be complete.' These words come from the last discourse of Christ our Lord in which he tells us of His own blessed intimacy with the Father and our sharing in that intimacy. 'As the Father has loved me so I have loved you. Abide in my love.'

Joy in His Sonship, in the Father's love for Him and His love for the Father was with Jesus even in the anguish of His mortal life, and it is now His in its fullness.

This blessed relationship of love we also share. We are God's sons and daughters, caught up in His heart, loved with an unspeakable love. This is our joy. Nothing can separate us from the love which comes to us in Christ Jesus our Lord. This joy can transcend anything the world can present in the way of pain and sorrow. 'In the world you will have trouble, but courage! the victory is mine; I have conquered the world!' Christ our Love and Lover has overcome the world which is at enmity with God. He has destroyed death and the powers of evil.

There can be no true joy until we can look death serenely in the face; and not only death as the instant which closes our mortal life but all those partial dyings which are ours and which wring our hearts. Such things as fear, pain, sickness and failing physical strength; traces of age on a beloved face, the last look at a place we love and shall never see again; every parting, every forgetfulness, just the sight of a fading flower – all these bring the breath of death and anguish to our sensitive hearts.

But faith in Jesus, the conqueror of death, in Jesus who, through His resurrection has given to all that seems negative and death-dealing a positive value, can enable us to rise above these afflictions and find true joy.

To some extent we can by numerous diversions and distractions keep at bay the experience of death which, without faith in Jesus, can eat away life's spirit; but such a state of peace and contentment would be superficial and could easily lead to callousness. We must pray to be granted gentle, loving, sensitive hearts, aware of the needs of others, and this means co-passion, co-suffering. Yet no suffering must rob us of joy. Always by faith we must see the power of the Resurrection at work.

Our joy must proclaim redemption and resurrection to the world. What greater witness can there be than a joy which transcends all pain? Our depths must be proclaiming that *nothing* can separate us from the love of Christ.

Let us try to open ourselves to the outpouring love and joy of the heart of God. The more we are filled with Him the more we will overflow to others. Let us pledge ourselves anew to this apostolate receiving God's love and letting it shine forth in our lives, then others will see and believe in the Father who reveals Himself in and through us.

The Lord is My Shepherd

We are a precious gift the Father has confided to Jesus. Thine they were: to me Thou gavest them. All that the Father gives me will come to me; and him that comes to me I will not cast out. This is the Father's will, that I should not lose one of these precious ones He has given to me. This charge which the Father has given me is more precious than anything whatsoever.

Jesus sees his own *raison d'être* as that of doing the will of the Father, and the will of the Father is precisely that He should care for each one of us and give us eternal life.

All that Jesus is is precisely for me. His care of me never slackens.

'The Lord is my shephered, I can want for nothing.' If I really believed this, how different my life would be! I would never willingly jib at what happens to me since I would see everything as at least permitted by Him, knowing He will make everything turn to my good. I would stop trying to run my own life, preventing this or that . . . I would cease to care for the judgements of others, whether they like me or not, whether they think well or ill of me. I would cease wanting to feel sure about everything, above all about my spiritual life: anxious, fearful, discouraged, plagued by guilt feelings ... If my faith in the unfailing tender care of my Shepherd is real, how could I allow such self-occupation?

The Shepherd psalm is one Jesus must have prayed a thousand and more times to His Father. 'The Lord carried you, as a man carries his child, all along the road you travelled.' ... at this hour you were led to the cross. Where are the nice green pastures on that stony and painful way? Where the still waters in His burning thirst? Did He feel His head and body were being washed and anointed with oil when the crown of thorns was pressing against His temples?

'He leads me along the right path: he is true to his name ... Surely goodness and kindness shall follow me all the days of my life.'

Had Jesus not held firmly to this certainty, that whatever it seemed or felt like this was the truth, the real nature of things, then we would not have been redeemed. His faith would have failed. But as it proved, His faith remained steadfast and triumphed.

The Good Shepherd is risen. He who laid down His life for the sheep, who died for His flock. He is risen. Alleluia!

Resurrection Faith

Here we see a little community busy with its day to day life. One of them is quicker than the others to perceive the Lord, to recognise Him in His hidden form. He tells the others. Peter apparently does not share this insight but he acts upon it immediately because he is so longing for Jesus. His heart recognises the note of truth in the other's announcement – there is no pride here. We can never overestimate our need of community if we are to live wholly for our Lord. We need the encouragement, the guidance and insights of others. Peter can't wait for the slow progress of the boat but jumps out and swims the remaining distance between himself and Jesus.

One of the great modern insights is the recognition of Christ in the secular. It was Bonhoeffer who gave challenging, public expression to it in his idea of religionless Christianity. In many instances this truly precious insight has led to profound error, denying the need for any 'sacred' activities whatever; neither liturgy, nor public or private prayer.

Rather, God is encountered in the neighbour and in secular life. This reaction to the sacral was needed and we have much to learn from it. But we must hold firmly in our hands the two strands of truth, and we can only do this if our faith is really deep.

If we truly believe in Jesus, then we live the whole of our lives, not bits and pieces of them, in that faith. Our attitudes, our evaluations, our judgements, our way of looking at things are wholly dependent on faith. Likewise all we think, say and do, our understanding of our duties, of what happens in the world, of art, books, and above all how we see and act towards people, reveal whether our faith is deep or not. We might put in a lot of time at prayer, might have deep thoughts and feelings about our Lord, might feel we would die for Him, and yet, in practice, we are perhaps 60 per cent, 90 per cent, agnostic.

The stormy colouring of this picture, which is yet suffused with a heavenly light, suggests the effort and turbulence of faith. Faith does not mean tranquillity in the ordinary sense; it does not mean a serene existence, it means conflict with darkness and doubt, struggle through blood and tears as with Jesus Himself, to be true to God.

CHRIST BY THE SEA OF GALILEE WITH PETER AND THE APOSTLES
Tintoretto

I Go to the Father

As we all know well, the Resurrection, Ascension and gift of the Holy Spirit are all one mystery looked at from different angles. The great mystery of reconciliation, the marriage between God and His creation, is split up for us in liturgical time to enable us to cope with it. The Ascension is not different from the Resurrection, rather we are asked to dwell on a partial aspect of the Resurrection.

The Ascension means essentially that Jesus is with His Father, 'I go to the Father'; and this is His supreme joy, His goal, His reward. 'If you loved me you would be full of joy because I am with my Father.' Are we? With a joy that can supersede all subjective states of trouble and grief?

The first aspect of the Ascension is unalloyed joy that no man can take away from us. The Father at last has all He wants – an open heart into which He can pour His love without hindrance. Jesus is the recipient of that blissful love, and we rejoice in Him and for Him.

Secondly, Jesus has entered heaven as our pioneer. He has

blazed a trail. More, He is our representative; in a real way
we are there with Him. The great work of reconciliation has
been accomplished. The massive dam walls that human
beings, through their wrong choices, had built up against
the love of God have been demolished. We have only to
stand in the way of these flood waters and not fly from them
as though fleeing from death.

'Abide in my love.' How do we abide in His love? He tells
us: 'If you keep my commandments you will abide in my
love, as it is by keeping my Father's commandments that I
abide in His love.' What we have seen Jesus doing in relation
to the Father, we must do. Jesus has shown us the Father
and what the Father wants of us; has shown us how we must
live to be in truth His children. We have to be living
embodiments of Jesus as He is of His Father. And this, says
Jesus, is my joy which you must share.

How the thought of the Ascension should lift our lives
above our petty, selfish concerns, to live with Jesus where
He is now – in the glory of the Father! That we are *able* to do
this, able to enter into the mystery of Jesus, to receive His
life and live by it, is the mystery of Pentecost.

Just as in Advent the Church invites us to assume the
attitude of those to whom the Lord has not yet come, and to
yearn for that coming, so now in the time between Ascension and Pentecost. We are invited to put ourselves with the
waiting disciples. Our ardent willing must hasten the coming of the Spirit, the Power from on high, who will enable
us to live the very life of Jesus.

Let us attend to Paul's exhortation:
    With unflagging energy,
    with ardour of spirit
    serve the Lord.
    Let hope keep you joyful,
    in trouble stand firm,
    persist in prayer.

Our Lady's Easter

At the moment of the Incarnation Christ Jesus became head of the human race. He redeemed us by His life, passion and death. Yet it was not until the Resurrection, when He was freed from all human limitations and transcended space and time that He entered fully into His office as Redeemer, Mediator, King. Then began His mystical indwelling in His Church and in every individual member of it.

In a similar way Mary became Mother of all men at the moment she became mother of Christ. By her intimate participation in His life, passion and death she became co-redemptrix. Yet not until her Assumption could she exercise fully her function of Queen, Mother and Mediatrix. Freed from the shackles of mortality she sees, knows, loves, protects, cares for each and all her children in a way we cannot comprehend.

We must never dissociate the two epochs: the earthly and the heavenly. Jesus is what He is because of His life on earth, because He fulfilled to the last iota the Father's will. So also

Mary is what she is because of her life on earth. The glory, the holiness, which now shines resplendant in heaven was forged here below. Her body, now set at the right hand of her Son, immersed in the Divine, was formed as is ours, from the dust, was nourished and grew to maturity by feeding on the bread and fruits of the earth, and by breathing the air we breathe. Her soul, as is ours, was perfected by the Holy Spirit – perfected by all she received through her senses, every event of her life, every joy that came her way, every sorrow.

Mary is true woman, blessed among women, fairest of womankind. Apart from the graces of her Divine Maternity and Immaculate Conception she was as we are; her supernatural life was like to ours. She lived by faith. She grew in grace and in the knowledge of God, grew in experience and in love, was ever learning. The simplicity, the ordinariness, the 'earthiness' of her life would seem to be incongruous with the glory she now enjoys: drawing water from a well, spinning, eating, sleeping . . . and heavenly bliss, communion with the Trinity! Something material has been taken up to the Holy of Holies, the sanctuary of the Divinity inaccessible to creatures!

Is it not rather more pertinent to say that Divinity has come down to earth, made His sanctuary in earth – earth has become heaven – the very dwelling place of God.

If we could see things as they really are I think we would see everything suffused with the Divine. Perhaps that is one of the profoundest lessons of the Assumption, and one which we all need to learn.

In our so-ordinary lives it is not easy to keep our spirits aloft, to sense the Divinity, to grasp the real value of events. Our calling is more beautiful than we could dream! Every day Christ is our Food – how that thought puts life in its proper perspective! Who am I that I need God to nourish me? What is this life that I live and which can only be sustained by the Lord Himself? What my dignity? What my destiny who feed upon God?

This age has been called the age of Mary. It is also, and indeed following on from that, the age of woman. More and more there seems to be a consciousness of woman's mission, woman's part in the salvation of our crumbling civilisation.

A woman's role is to be, to live, to receive. Mary perfectly expressed that role: '*Fiat mihi*' – be it done to me. But this is no mere passivity; it is the *willed* receiving, the *willed* embracing, the *willed* cherishing, the *willed* sacrifice of self to bring forth life.

Imagine if you can Mary's joy on Easter morn when she saw the Divine Seed she had borne within herself now risen and glorious – *surget sicut lilium*. The grain of wheat falling into her furrow had died, (for though He left her womb He never left her heart) and how has burgeoned anew, the first fruits of a vast harvest.

So it is with us. We can be sure. Let us then remain humble, faithful, patient under the hand of God. '*Fiat mihi*'. Hereafter we shall see the harvest. Meanwhile let us be content to wait. May Mary our mother teach us perfect motherhood which is all self-donation, self-giving to Christ and His Church. This is the essence of the Christian woman's vocation.

Varia

I Am the Bread of Life

On the feast of Corpus Christi we are asked to exult in the precious gift of the Blessed Sacrament. Our Lord is present in the liturgical gathering, present everywhere in the Spirit, present in each sacrament. Nevertheless we can see the Blessed Sacrament as His presence *par excellence*, a sign of the constant nearness of the Risen Lord.

He is the immolated One, the One who gave, and gives, Himself. His abiding presence under the sacramental bread is a sign of our union with Him and His abiding within us.

The Mass is the action whereby we make present the immolated, surrendered One, and enter into His self-offering.

The Blessed Sacrament is this action 'held'. It is always a window onto the Mass, onto the surrender of Jesus. The Blessed Sacrament is always inviting us 'Take eat ... my Body for you'. He is there to be eaten, to be the life whereby I live. He is always there to tell me that I cannot live my day out of my own resources but only in Him.

I can perhaps forget my Mass. But each time I come before the Blessed Sacrament I am forcibly reminded of it – His Body, given for my life through His death.

The living Christ communicates through His risen corporality. He is Man. The only way we can give ourselves is through our bodies, we *are* body.

Our work is an expression of love, an expression of our self-giving. In personal relationships too love must be manifest in bodily form, else it has no reality for the other.

Love must be incarnated, and so we need not only action but also tender intimacies. We need to hunger for the Eucharist as did the saints. Then Jesus will transform us into His own life – Life given, Life Risen.

Heart of the Saviour

This is, I think, one of the profoundest feasts of the year. The Church has just led us through the great Paschal cycle, instructing the mind, opening the heart to the graces of redemption: what redemption means, what God has done for us, how we must receive fully the redemption already gained for us.

After the feast of Pentecost the Church puts before us another Holy Thursday when, in a different atmosphere, we contemplate again the mystery of the Eucharist. Then she puts before us another Good Friday when we concentrate on a Heart, the Heart of God, and that Heart is shown to us as both pierced and burning. She is trying to do the impossible, trying to give expression to the overwhelming love of God revealed in Jesus crucified. The Heart of Jesus is the very Heart of God reconciling us to Himself.

I am going to try to speak of the ineffable, to do the impossible in saying something of Jesus or, to keep to the precise imagery of the feast which is important, the Heart of

Jesus. This will be done under three headings.

The Heart of Jesus is the Heart of God. To see him is to see the invisible, incomprehensible Father, infinite Mystery. The mystery of love which is God has always sought to share Himself, to bring men to a knowledge and love of Himself in which lies their sole fulfilment. In times past, in diverse ways, throughout the aeons, there have been men and women of whom we know nothing who have opened themselves to the Mystery and come to true knowledge. Others we know; we read of them in the Old Testament. Here is a book, or collection of books, recording men's search after knowledge of God which is seen truly to be God's search to reveal Himself. We know we can light upon wonderful passages: Isaiah, Jeremiah, Hosea, Job . . . and we see that here, this particular individual was in the truth. Here is true insight, true knowledge, wholly conforming to the Father Jesus reveals to us. They stand out amid so much that is not the pure, lovely face of the Father but man's distorted image of Him; the image sinful, selfish man fashions for himself.

What strikes me forcibly is that it is individuals alone who come to this inner knowledge. A whole people can have the right words, the right images; but the inner knowledge is missing and so the very words and images, once so shining and pure, become distorted. If we look closely at a few men who attained knowledge of God in some degree we shall see it was always through personal crucifixion, their own hearts pierced.

Hosea is a familiar example of how, through his own most painful experience and loving response he arrived at an understanding of the Heart of God. Let us look at two others, Moses and David. For Moses the incident I allude to is when, returning from his intimate encounter with God on the mountain, bearing the tablets of the commandments, he finds the people succumbing to idolatory. His anger burns with frustration and a sense of outrage and he seems to hear God saying: 'I have seen this people and behold it is a stiff-necked people. Now therefore let me alone that my wrath may burn hot against them and I may consume them; but of you I will make a great nation.' Moses' heart, wounded as it is, is still more outraged by this word. Can this be the God, the Saviour God who pledged Himself to save His people? Could such a One take such an attitude? Moses' pure heart answered 'No' – not in a theoretical way but by the sacrifice of his own anger and his surrender to compassion and forgiveness. He knew God by acting like Him. His own response *is* the knowledge of God: 'Alas, this people have sinned a great sin . . . but now forgive them their sin – if not, blot me out I pray you from the book of life.' Thus Moses learned by *doing* that 'the Lord is a God merciful and gracious, slow to anger and abounding in steadfast love and faithfulness, forgiving iniquity and transgressions'. Yet he is not a soft, undemanding God. Far from it!

Look at David when, at the end of his life, as a very old man he loses everything through the treachery of his son Absalom. David learned something about God in this time of betrayal and desolation that he never learned in his astute heyday. You remember how his faithful followers mustered an army to defeat the treacherous uprising, and seemingly David's sole concern was for the arch traitor, Absalom. 'For my sake protect the young man Absalom.' We know the sequence. Joab and his men, following the dictates of commonsense, ignore the old king's sentimental wishes and slay the dangerous troublemaker. News of the great victory and the restoration of all he has lost is brought to the king waiting at the gate. He isn't interested. He has only one question, one concern: 'Is it well with the young man Absalom?' And the king was deeply moved and went to the chamber over the gate, weeping his heart out for the worthless son who had so wronged him: 'O my son Absalom, my son, my son! Would that I had died instead of you, O Absalom my son, my son!'

Thus David, through intense suffering patiently and lovingly borne, not governed by the dictates of human standards, commonsense, justice, listens only to the still, small voice of the Spirit within, prompting incessant love and forgiveness. His own heart mirrors the Heart of God.

The story of the Prodigal Son, the lost sheep, the apparent unconcern for the ninety-nine tell the same story. The accent in these parables is not on 'the others' but on the '*one*' – the profound love, compassion, forgiveness for you, for me . . . not for crowds. And it is above all, in Jesus, that we see God's Heart, and the knowledge of that Heart is communicated to us.

This Heart is a pierced Heart. Jesus stands before us with a pierced Heart. We have seen how knowledge of God has always cost; the human heart has to be broken open before it can receive God, and thus it was with Jesus. And the deepest mystery of all is that we learn that the Father's own Heart is pierced.

How can we enter into this pierced heart? Only by becoming like it, living in love at whatever cost, paying the high price of loving. Too easily we assume that loving is a pleasurable experience. Most surely it is the only sweetness in life but this must be understood correctly. True love is always bleeding in our mortal life. You simply cannot have love in this life without pain.

Just think of our own way of carrying on. We get hurt, offended . . . what do we do? Shrink into ourselves, erect all sorts of barriers. Our heart has withdrawn from the one who hurts us in any way. We mustn't be hurt, 'I matter', our poor ego cries. But that is not how Jesus loves. If we would be like Him we must struggle to the death with all this – refuse to curl up, refuse to withdraw in the slightest. We must go on exposing ourselves, giving ourselves, pouring ourselves out.

We say we want to love, we want to serve, we want to give ourselves, and at bottom we are saying we want selfish satisfaction. We want to feel we matter, are important, we want to feel fulfilled; in other words we are using others, and the beautiful concept of love is being abused. Love is selfless. The way into the Heart of Jesus is not through intellectual insight, not through glowing emotion, but through learning to pay the cost of pure love. There is sacrifice involved in letting others be themselves.

It is a Heart on fire. This Heart is burning. Nothing could stop Jesus ascending the mountain to God: on, on he pressed, bleeding, exhausted. So must we. Again, it isn't a question of burning emotion but of burning determination, resolution to give God everything, saying 'Yes, Yes' to every new demand of the God who draws us up relentlessly to our supreme fulfilment in Himself.

So this feast is saying: 'Look long, look hard at this pierced and burning Heart, and respond.'

'Come to me,' cries Jesus 'I will give you rest.' I don't know about you, but for me, to speak of eternal joy, delight, bliss, is unreal. I simply cannot imagine unalloyed joy and delight engulfing the whole of me. I know joy, but it is that of sacrifice, of loving God at cost; this is the only joy that means anything to me. But when I think of the more modest term 'rest' – yes, then my heart responds. To be at rest: yearning, struggle, empty longing filled . . . yes, this means something. I will give you rest because I give you the Father; and you come to Me by taking my yoke upon yourself, the yoke of humble, meek, devoted loving. This is to know the Father, the God of all-compassion.

A Bridal Response

Religious life means nothing if not a bridal relationship with God. Our deepest, our only motivation for being in Carmel, must be that of a total response to love.

In Jesus we are bidden to look at the pierced heart of the Saviour with all that it suggests of absolute love, perfect sacrifice. We are bidden to see this heart as a source, a fountain pouring out all that is good, best, sweetest – all that we need for our blessedness. We are bidden to listen to His inconceivable invitation – 'Come to me ... for rest, for comfort. Come to me to drink, I am all that you need for perfect fulfilment.'

In God's plan marriage to the man she loves is meant to bring a woman to her completion. Jesus is our Man. We must pour out on Him the devotion of our lives, really make Him the object of our love; our thoughts always turning to Him, our choices and decisions made in His light. If we trust Him utterly, staking everything on Him, basing ourselves on His love, His fidelity, then all He has told us He is for us, all He has promised He will do for us, will BE.

To think of our Lord as being able to grieve can become one of our strongest motivations towards loving Him. There is a divine Heart to grieve, and if it were not for Jesus we could not know this fact. The fundamental thing we learn from Him is that God is self-bestowal, He is all generosity, all heart.

Because Jesus has given Himself wholly to God, God has given Himself wholly to Jesus. The ultimate of God's self-bestowal is here.

The risen Lord is now triumphant in joy, nothing is unaccomplished in Him, He has allowed Himself to be broken open by love, and has become the source of this same love – for us. But, He bears the marks of His wounds, His heart is still pierced, because we, His brethren, are not yet fulfilled in love.

Being called to Carmel means the vocation to live out intensely, for all, the human destiny to be, with Jesus, a capacity for God's self-giving. We don't have to be talented, only utterly faithful and ready to give all. But how often we heedlessly reject this love, preferring ourselves instead.

Let us enter fully into that death to self which is, in reality, a death burning with life. Fixing our eyes on Jesus we shall find courage for everything, knowing that our Man has a heart we can grieve, or a heart we can delight.

Sustained Passion

'It is not the strength but the duration of great desires that makes great men.'

Few saints are better known than St Teresa. Her books, her letters, self-revealing as they are, are widely read. But perhaps there is a kind of knowledge proper to those who actually live according to the life-style her genius planned. This is not to claim that it is a higher, deeper knowledge but simply that it is different perhaps from what can be gained from her writings alone. Not only her books but the actual thing that evolved as she put her hand to giving new form, new direction to the ancient Rule of St Albert, reveals what manner of woman she was. The Carmel of her devising, the child of her spirit, is a kind of replica or mirror, not only of her spirit but of her human characteristics also. She put her whole self into it; it was born of her profound spiritual insight which, in turn, was wedded to her natural gifts and temperament. As an historian can reconstruct an earlier civilisation from its present-day descendants, so, in the measure that Carmel is authentic, we could recapture Teresa without her written works.

A truly amazing feature of Teresa's work of reform is its sureness. Right from the start she knew what she wanted. There was no groping towards some dim vision. No, it was there, clear and shining. Of course details had to be worked out, tried, modified, changed, but the main structure, together with the inner motivation and direction, were there from the beginning. Teresa attributes this certitude to God himself. She describes in the *Life* how it came about that she undertook her great work. Though for some time she had been dissatisfied with the way of life at the Incarnation, it seems not to have entered her head to do anything so radical, as, in fact, she did.

'One day it happened that a person to whom I was talking, with some other sisters, asked me why we should not become Discalced nuns, for it would be quite possible to find a way of establishing a convent.' (*Life* 32) This was the voice of extreme youth, the middle-aged Teresa was more reserved. 'I had had desires of this kind myself so I began to discuss the matter with a companion . . . But for my own part, I was most happy in the house where I was, for I was fond both of the house and of my cell, and this held me back.' (ibid)

Then comes what she was convinced was the divine intervention. It was after Communion. 'The Lord gave me the most explicit commands to work for this aim with all my might and main and made me wonderful promises . . . that the convent would be a star giving out the most brilliant light.' (ibid) Thus an idea which she had toyed with but with no determination or certainty, becomes an irresistible obsession. The certitude that God wills her to found a

convent of perfect observance is the source of her indefatig-
able determination and drive. The certitude never dies. She
understands that God has a dream and Carmel in its perfection is that dream. The Carmel that is to come into being is
of immense importance to God, it is to have a vital role in
the Church. How could she hesitate, how could she spare
herself or compromise?

'With zeal I have been zealous for the honour of my
Spouse, Jesus Christ, who spoke to me: "You must be truly
my spouse consumed with zeal for my honour".' (Liturgy)
If one were looking for a key-word to describe Teresa, it
would be, I think, 'passion'. It is one thing to speak of love
and another of passion. We say of someone, 'he loves
music'; of another, 'music is his passion'. Passion implies
obsession; all-consuming, devouring one's time, energy,
one's whole substance. This surely is the meaning of 'zeal'.
We are looking now at the later Teresa when she had broken
free of her self and her binding attachment and was literally
consumed with love, with passion, and it is this passion that
is the characteristic of Carmel, not the passion of an hour, of
a day but of a whole lifetime – sustained passion. Without
passion Carmel is not Carmel, it is a dead thing, a mediocre
existence deprived of the best human values. Carmel must
be all or nothing. It has to be lived to the full or else it is a
pitiable existence. Teresa herself recognises this.

> This house is another heaven if it be possible to have
> heaven on earth. Anyone whose sole pleasure lies in
> pleasing God and who cares nothing for her own plea-
> sure will find our life a very good one; if she wants
> anything more, she will lose everything, for there is
> nothing more to be had. (*Way* 13)

Into this work of reform Teresa poured all her powers,

physical, psychic, spiritual, to provide our Lord with utterly true friends who would make His concerns their own and would cease to care at all for themselves. What was true of her was to become true of those chosen for Carmel. 'O my Jesus! If one could but describe how great a gain it is to cast ourselves into the arms of this Lord and make an agreement with His Majesty that I should look to my Beloved and He towards me, that He would take care of my affairs and I of His.' (*Conceptions* 4) They were to make it their sole aim to carry out the teaching of Jesus with the greatest perfection for 'You are my friends if you do what I command you.' They were to study to know this teaching, to know the will of God, the mind of Christ. This is the burden of her teaching, not how to distinguish one mystical state from another, but how to imitate Jesus, how to live with his life. The 'choice' souls who aspire to Carmel must be seeking 'all perfection'; they have received a spark of love which, if fostered, will burst into a flame of passion. Teresa designed the way of life so that everything should converge onto fanning this spark and there is no place in Carmel for what does not press towards passion.

The efficacy, the sanctifying power of Carmel lies in holding in fine balance two seemingly opposing elements, the eremetical and community. There are all the advantages of solitude without its drawbacks; all the advantages of community, carefully controlled to ensure its total Christlikeness. Teresa's understanding of a way that is wholly eremitical in spirit yet lived in community ('yet' is misleading, community is the means of acquiring the truly eremitical heart which is to be alone with God alone) sprang directly from her own experience.

It had been her lot to make her painful ascent to God in an unsupportive community. Far from helping her to give herself to God, it hampered her, indulging her weaknesses. For twenty years she struggled, falling and rising, and eventually won through to a decisive determination to let God have everything. Thus passion was born.

> I desired, therefore, to flee from others and to end by withdrawing myself completely from the world. My spirit was restless, yet the restlessness was not disturbing but pleasant: I knew quite well that it was of God and that His Majesty had given my soul this ardour to enable me to digest other and stronger meat than I had hitherto been in the habit of eating. (*Life* 32)
> Do Thou strengthen and prepare my soul first of all, Good of all good, my Jesus, and do Thou then ordain means whereby I may do something for Thee, for no one could bear to receive as I have done and pay nothing in return ... now that I have approached Thee, now that I have mounted this watch-tower whence truths can be seen, I shall be able to do all things provided Thou withdraw not from me. (ibid 21)

She has a strong desire for solitude not so as to enjoy it (for her, 'it is most important for souls when they begin to practice prayer to start by detaching themselves from every kind of pleasure, and to enter upon their prayer with one sole determination, to help Christ bear His Cross') (ibid 15) but as a way of giving herself more purely to God. She sees that for her to live her Rule perfectly is to help the world Jesus died for.

Teresa, setting out to found a house, and later houses, in which the Rule of St Albert was to be kept in its pristine perfection, freely and definitely chose a very strict enclosure. It was not just a concession to the times, to the legislation of the Council of Trent; she chose it as essential for the particular vocation of prayer to which she knew herself called by God and which was to be the vocation of all who would follow her into Carmel. Teresita, her niece, who had entered Carmel very young, testified many years later to what Teresa herself had early outlined to her brother, 'they will live in the strictest enclosure, never going out, and seeing no one without having veils over their faces. . . .' (Letter 2)

> She (Teresita) said that she knew it was the holy Mother Teresa of Jesus who had started the Order called that of the Discalced Carmelites and that she had been moved to do so by a desire for the glory of God our Lord and for the good of souls. She wished to try to live and to get others to live in the closest possible seclusion and to keep their vows by means of poverty and penance. (Appendix 6)

It would be easy on a superficial reading of Teresa's activities, the countless letters she wrote, the vast number of people she knew, to conclude that she had one standard of enclosure for herself and another for her nuns. This was not so. If we look carefully we shall see how set she was on seclusion. The uncomfortable journeys were made even more uncomfortable – tormenting at times – by her insistence that the carts should be covered so that she and her little band of nuns might spend the time as if they were in enclosure. At stopping places on the way, in lodgings to which they had recourse when they could not immediately take over the house of their choice, she went to elaborate pains to establish some sort of enclosure appointing one sister to answer the door. Inevitably the business of her foundations took her out; inevitably it was more often for her than for the other nuns, but she was realistic, she knew that they could lose in a way she could not now for they were mostly young and certainly young in the ways of pure love and detachment.

Teresa could have pushed the seclusion on the individual

level also. She could have founded a complex of cells with the inmates meeting only rarely – after all, this would have been more in line with the primitive Rule she was restoring. With amazing freedom she acted differently insisting on a strong community life. Hours of solitude, yes, but Liturgy, meals, recreation daily together. It is this latter that must give us pause. She arranged that her hermits should come together twice a day to talk to one another! To understand, let us look again at Teresa's own life. She had experienced the spiritual harm that comes from a lax enclosure, from a worldly community, true, but she had also experienced the indispensable benefits of living with others in community. The difficulties she had had to contend with, the struggle to be kind, uncritical, serviceable, truly obedient and humble, were what forged her sanctity. Not only the negative factors: she was immensely helped by others. Friendship had played a vital role in her spiritual development, to throw this overboard would have been tempting God. He had enlightened her and helped her in countless ways through others and she grasped vividly that this is his normal means. How well she writes of this, drawn from her own experience.

> It is here, my daughters, that love is to be found, not hidden away in corners but in the midst of occasions of sin; and believe me, although we may often fail and commit small lapses, our gain will be incomparably greater . . . The reason I say we gain more . . . is that it makes us realise what we are and of how much our own nature is capable. For if a person is always recollected, however holy he may think himself to be, he does not know if he is patient and humble, and has no means of knowing it. (*Foundations* 5)

What Teresa is doing is controlling the environment for

her nuns. Their vocation is to live in the greatest possible concentration, to spend their whole lives in prayer for the salvation of the world. To do this effectively their psychic and spiritual energies must be conserved. Enclosure ensures this can be done. They are preserved from the incessant bombardment of persons and things, each calling for a response. For those whose vocation is to live 'in the world' this is the way they encounter God – a demanding vocation calling for supreme vigilance, generosity and prayer. The Carmelite's way is different. The emphasis in her life is to receive God so that she may give Him; being there before Him as an empty river-bed receiving his waters with which the world can be irrigated. But she cannot be this empty river-bed, cannot be 'there' for him unless she is 'clean of heart'. Solitude in itself is nothing. We are no closer to God in physical solitude than in physical proximity to others. To be alone with God alone means an utterly pure surrendered heart and the only way to this is through the purification of learning to live with others and loving them. So, though the environment is carefully protected from randomness, it contains within itself everything necessary for human purification and development. It is a little world of its own and amazingly rich thanks to the rich personality of Teresa.

The Carmelite very soon finds herself 'up against it'. Because everything is streamlined, cut down to a minimum, because there are no diversions and the focus is intense, 'occasions of sin', as present as in the world, should be more quickly recognised and more summarily dealt with. Within the small world of a Carmelite enclosure there circulate all the emotions and desires of the human heart. Like everyone else who would be a true christian, the Carmelite has to fight to the death, struggling with her selfishness at every turn, with her ambition, her desire to be successful, esteemed, important. She has to learn to live in submission, for true obedience is a service of love to the community and a drastic surgery to the self-centred ego. She has long hours of unoccupied prayer where, exposed to God, she entreats for light and strength; she has times for being with others whether at work or at recreation when the opportunities arise for the practice of virtue in imitation of 'His Majesty'. There is no other way, declares Teresa, over and over again. She knows from her own experience that there isn't. Perfect love of the neighbour which demands utter humility and self-forgetfulness, is all that matters. Some wound to self-love is inflicted or we have our shabbiness shown up and there is no escape, for back we must go to the solitude and there learn to accept 'humble self-knowledge'. 'I think it is a greater favour if the Lord sends us a single day of self-knowledge, even at the cost of many afflictions and trials, than many days of prayer.' (*Foundations* 5)

This passionate lover would have her daughters give everything, be constantly vigilant so that nothing escapes them, no word, no deed, no idle thought indulged. Teresa's passion is never up in the air but always brought down to earth, to concrete expressions of loving desire, affirming in very fact, 'You are all I desire'. 'Never speak without thinking well of what you are going to say and commending it earnestly to our Lord lest you say anything displeasing to Him . . . Never exaggerate . . . Never affirm anything unless you are sure it is true'. Teresa was especially concerned with truthfulness and lamented a lack of straight forwardness: 'The prioress is shrewder than befits her vocation . . . she has never been frank with me', and to Gratian himself, addressing him in the third person, 'I was wondering if he is not rather careless sometimes in telling the truth about everything . . . I should like him to be extremely careful about it . . . I do not believe there can be absolute perfection where there is carelessness about that.'

All that Teresa had learned over the long, painful years,

she urged on her daughters, little things perhaps and yet so very important if we would be wholly God's.

> Do not pander to your curiosity by talking or asking questions about things which do not concern you . . . Do not eat or drink save at the proper times . . . Do not complain about food . . . Always do what those in your community bid you, if it is not contrary to obedience, and answer them with humility and gentleness . . . Never do anything you could not do in the sight of all . . . Take great care over your nightly examen . . . In all you do and at all times examine your conscience, and having seen your faults, strive with the Divine help to amend them; by following this course you will attain perfection.

A Carmelite must be completely detached from herself so that she is free for love. Unless she works for this with all her might and main, making it the passion of her life, there is no point in the enclosed life – Teresa has said so herself.

To be a true friend of Jesus Christ, to share his intimate secrets, to be transformed in him, this is the aim Teresa set for her Carmels. Enclosed in body, the heart of the Carmelite is to be as vast as the heart of Christ. We can watch Teresa labouring for love like this throughout her life. A thoughtful reading of her letters awes one with the impression of a self-expenditure which was complete. This is perfect imitation of Him who is total expenditure. Those marvellous letters, each one distinct, each framed for the recipient with a delicacy only Christ-like love and respect could engender. She can exhort her daughters:

> Try, then, sisters, to be as pleasant as you can, without offending God, and get on as well as you can with those you have to deal with so that they may like

talking to you and want to follow your way of life and conversation and not be frightened and put off by virtue. This is very important for nuns: the holier they are the more sociable they should be with their sisters.

The first field for the exercise of this selfless love is within the community itself. Thus they would comfort, support and enlighten one another, making it easy for one another to love God. The prioress must give leave 'when one sister wishes to speak to another about their Spouse in order to quicken their love for Him, or to comfort her if she is in some necessity or temptation.' A Teresian Carmel is a happy, gracious dwelling, but – let there be no mistake – at the price of constant effort and sacrifice; if they are like their Mother, their love will be so easy, so gracious as to seem effortless and natural. But it cost her as it must cost us all and she tells us that it was a constant trial to her 'putting up with people of so many different temperaments'.

This love within the community must flow outside, covering the whole world with its prayers but specifically touching with its radiance individuals who have contact in one way or another with the monastery. 'Fall in with the mood of the person to whom you are speaking. Be happy with those who are happy and sad with those who are sad' . . . 'don't worry about his being upset: he is always like that. Keep him as friendly as you can.'

A striking feature of her great charity displayed artlessly in her letters, is her forgiveness. She would allow no 'bad feeling' to exist even with a person who had no great call upon her. She would put herself to a lot of trouble to mollify, sweeten, heal and not just for diplomacy – though undeniably this was there at times, but for sheer, gracious love. Her own daughters wounded her but how generously she overlooked the hurt and continued to show the same openheartedness, exposing herself and her weakness to them. When one considers how young they were both in years and in religious life, it is all the more impressive.

> Where they go wrong, it seems to me, is that, while I put so much love and care into everything that concerns them, they fail in their duty by paying no heed to me and letting me tire myself out in vain. It was because I felt like that I got angry, and would have nothing more to do in the matter, thinking, as I said, that I was doing no good, as indeed is the case. But such is love that I felt, if my words could be of no avail, I could not wash my hands at all. (*Letters*)

It could well be that the constant nausea, weakness and blinding headaches Teresa endured were a direct effect of this unflagging involvement. We could often see, writes one of her daughters,

> ... to our great distress, what inroads they made upon her strength of body. Although these assaults were interior ones, they were of such a kind as to leave many marks upon the body ... She told me about this several times after it was all over and said that, whenever she saw such a soul improving and making progress, she knew she would have to pay for it.

Teresa wanted her Carmelites to sacrifice themselves continually for the world. Strictest enclosure yet infinite concern. 'Do not let your soul dwell in seclusion, or, instead of acquiring holiness, you will develop many imperfections, which the devil will implant in you in other ways, in which case, as I have said, you will not do the good you might, either to yourself or to others.' (*Way* 14) She praises the prioresses who are concerned for the Order as a whole whereas she reproaches one for being wrapped up in her own community:

> You know I dislike the way all of you think no one can see things as your Reverence can: that, as I say, is because you are concerned only with your own community and not with things that affect many other communities as well . . . It is a great mistake to think you know everything, and then say you are humble. You do not look beyond the limits of your own house. (*Letters*)

A ladylike, leisurely existence was not Teresa's idea of Carmel. It was to be a life of hard work for her nuns profess poverty and the poor must work for their living. Teresa would seem to have been possessed of incredible energy. She was carrying the burden of the foundations, interesting herself deeply in the affairs of her family since she had no option, and the affairs of many others who had recourse to her charity, all this involving constant letter-writing into the small hours of the morning. On top of this her books. Even so, she did not exempt herself from the remunerative work she strongly imposed upon her communities. She was spinning whenever she had a spare moment and would take her distaff to the parlour with her for, after all, the fingers can still be busy while one is talking even on lofty spiritual matters! Even if a particular convent does not need the income from our work, the sisters must work every bit as hard and give away what they do not need to poorer houses. Like the truly poor they must be satisfied with a minimum, the simplest of food, clothing, furnishings. In actual fact both she and her nuns were often cold and hungry. Teresa would darn and patch her own clothing to make it last as long as she could. On being sent a freize habit, 'I am most grateful to her as my other was too full of holes for the cold weather . . .' it seems 'Our Father (Gratian) had forcibly to take it from her.' (*Letters*).

This outward detachment must be the natural expression of a detached heart. Not the slightest thing may be one's own and 'if a sister is seen to be attached to anything, the prioress must be very careful to take it from her, whether it be a book, or a cell or whatever else'. (*Constitutions*) Teresa's own evangelical spirit is reflected in her Carmel: contentment with little, generous human effort, but then no anxiety, only perfect confidence in God who will supply all that is necessary.

Narrowness, rigidity, pettiness, infantilism, these must have no place in these dovecots of our Lady. They must house 'royal souls'. 'I find a puerility in that house which is intolerable'. She wants her daughters to be mature women even though she often finds they are not. She was not afraid of her rich womanliness; she realised it was with this she loved our Lord, he positively wanted it, and this same capacity she trained her nuns to acquire. They must abandon childishness and become 'strong men'. Whilst abhorring pretension she admired intelligence, 'it is a great advantage in every way to be intelligent.' (*Foundations*) She was proud of her daughters capabilities and administrative gifts – no slovenliness in her houses as to arrangements, running or keeping of accounts! Her prioresses, young though they are, must act with maturity: 'never take a step without asking many people's opinion, and thinking things over very carefully' and 'they must not think they can first give an order and then countermand it . . .' (*Letters*) as if they were a capricious worldly mistress dealing with her servants.

Other would-be saints have thought fit to mar what they felt to be an alluring and therefore dangerous beauty. Not Teresa. She took delight in physical beauty and charm of manner, though never, of course, giving them undue im-

portance. As everyone testifies, she was a veritable heart-
stealer herself, of immense charm and well she knew it. It
did not occur to her to dim its radiance, to act in an uncouth
way. On the contrary, she used it to the full and took
thought and trouble to act with human lovableness to win
people to a life of goodness. She tells her prioresses that they
must strive to make themselves loved, not for their own
sake, but so as to make the yoke of obedience easier for their
sisters. A fine sense of humour she had too, and this she has
bequeathed to her family. 'God deliver us from sour-faced
saints!' Has anyone of you a gift for entertaining? Let her use
it to the full. Store up funny stories with which to amuse a
sick sister. Teresa was quick to see the comic and quick with
a witty response, and she could subtly correct faults by
gentle satire, 'leg-pulling'. 'Your Reverence is getting what
you wanted. God forgive you! Pray to Him that my coming may be good for you and make you less attached to
getting your own way. I do not think this is possible, but
God can do everything.' Her humour breaks forth in ex-
asperation to Gratian when she tells him to stop dithering
'or you will be the death of me!' (*Letters*)

Within the limitations of her times she wanted her daughters to be well-instructed and in contact with the finest
theological minds in Spain. She was not averse to them
taking an interest in local and national events provided these
were a help to prayer. The Moriscos of Seville were plotting
revolution:

> Find out the rights of this and ask Mother Subprioress
> to write and tell us about it ... They (the sisters of
> Segovia), think it is a fine thing to be in the middle of all
> those flags and excitements if you can profit by all the
> news you must be getting and extract some spiritual
> profit from it; but it is most important for you to
> consider very carefully how you are to behave or you

will find it distracting. I long for you all to be very holy. (*Letters*)

Teresa herself had a child's sense of wonder and a vibrant interest in the human scene and her daughters may have the same. If possible – and she was prepared to pay for the privilege – she wanted to provide them with a big garden and lovely views. 'Do you think it is a small advantage to have a house from which you can see the galleys go by? We envy you all here, for it is a great help towards praising God. I assure you, if your nuns are deprived of it their praises will suffer.' (*Letters*) Teresa would never play the 'saint': her energies and attention were completely absorbed elsewhere. It is evident that, in her life time, her daughters did not think of their 'old mother' as a *saint*! One gets the impression that, at times, they found her a bit in the way and, incredible though it seems to us, were willing to set their judgement against hers – young prioresses longing to try out their own wings. She exposed herself so nakedly to them, readily revealing her failing, her loneliness, her weakness, her need of love. This sort of thing could blind the unenlightened to her sanctity, it's all just 'too human'. 'How oppressed I have been lately, but the oppression passed when I heard that you were well'. And the pathetic lament to Gratian in her deep hurt and disappointment with the nun she so deeply loved: 'She should realise I am not such a bad christian. In such a grave matter, people living a long way off should not speak against one who would give up her own peace of mind for the good and tranquillity of a single soul.' (*Letters*) And she can readily express her sorrow for hastiness: 'I wish I had not made them (trials) worse for you. Your Reverence must pardon me, but when I really love anyone, I am so anxious she should not go astray that I am unbearable.' In a different vein, she gaily admits that she enjoyed a journey – because of the company! 'How well I remember what a good time he (Gratian, of course) and I had together on the journey from Toledo to Avila, which did not do me any harm'. Such disarming exposure is open to misunderstanding and to abuse but Teresa was heedless of that; this was her way of giving herself.

Visitors to Carmel are often startled by the down-to-earthness, the naturalness, gaiety and spontaneity they find, a reaction that quickly turns to delight. This is an inheritance from their rich, womanly Mother.

Teresa died and there passed away 'a glory from the earth'. It need not be so: her inspiration, her passion formed a structure, a way of life which, surrendered to, will engender this same glorious thing. Sustained passion burning at the heart of the world: not an emotion but a constant, ever renewed determination to let God be God, to have simply everything, to be one with 'His glorious Son' receiving the fulness of the Spirit.